german art of the twentieth century

german art of the twentieth century

by Werner Haftmann   Alfred Hentzen   William S. Lieberman

edited by Andrew Carnduff Ritchie

The Museum of Modern Art, New York

in collaboration with The City Art Museum of St. Louis, Missouri

distributed by Simon and Schuster, New York

Published by the Museum of Modern Art, New York, 1957
All rights reserved
Library of Congress Catalogue Card Number 57-11679
Typography by Charles Oscar; cover design by Otl Aicher
Printed in Germany by Brüder Hartmann, Berlin

Lenders to the Exhibition

Otto Baum, Esslingen; Walter Bareiss, Greenwich, Connecticut; Mrs. Margarete Baumeister, Stuttgart; Mr. and Mrs. Erich Cohn, New York; Mr. and Mrs. Bruce B. Dayton, Minneapolis, Minnesota; Richard L. Feigen, New York; Mrs. W. Feilchenfeldt, Zurich, Switzerland; Dr. Max Fischer, Stuttgart; Andrew P. Fuller, Fort Worth, Texas; Kurt H. Grunebaum, Harrison, New York; Dr. Hugo Häring, Biberach an der Riss; Mrs. Gabriel Hauge, Washington, D. C.; Max Kruss, Berlin; Dr. Stephan Lackner, Santa Barbara, California; Mrs. Gisela Macke, Bonn; Mr. and Mrs. Samuel H. Maslon, Wayzata, Minnesota; Mr. and Mrs. Morton D. May, St. Louis, Missouri; Mrs. Gertrud A. Mellon, New York; Mr. and Mrs. Morton Neumann, Chicago; Mrs. Hanna Bekker-vom Rath, Frankfurt; Nelson A. Rockefeller, New York; Dr. and Mrs. Allan Roos, New York; Walther Scharf, Oberstdorf/Allgäu; Herman Shulman Collection, New York; Dr. Bernhard Sprengel, Hanover; Hans Uhlmann, Berlin; Mr. and Mrs. Richard K. Weil, St. Louis, Missouri; Fritz Winter, Diessen/Ammersee; Dr. Ferdinand Ziersch, Wuppertal-Barmen; Mr. and Mrs. Frederick Zimmermann, New York.

Ehemals Staatliche Museen Berlin, National-Gallery; Kunsthalle, Bremen; Albright Art Gallery, Buffalo; The Art Institute of Chicago; Wallraf-Richartz Museum, Cologne; The Detroit Institute of Arts, Michigan; Städtisches Museum, Duisburg; Kunstsammlungen der Stadt Düsseldorf; Stedelijk van Abbe-museum, Eindhoven, Holland; Folkwang Museum, Essen; Kunsthalle, Hamburg; Niedersächsische Landesgalerie, Hanover; Staatliche Kunsthalle, Karlsruhe; Walker Art Center, Minneapolis, Minnesota; Bayerische Staatsgemäldesammlungen, Munich; The Solomon R. Guggenheim Museum, New York; Smith College Museum of Art, Northampton, Massachusetts; Philadelphia Museum of Art, Pennsylvania; Portland Art Museum, Oregon; Saarland Museum, Saarbrücken; City Art Museum of St. Louis, Missouri; Staatliche Kunstsammlungen, Stuttgart; Kunsthaus, Zurich, Switzerland; Fine Arts Associates, New York; Rose Fried Gallery, New York; Kleemann Galleries, New York.

contents

for Curt Valentin

foreword

The exhibition accompanying this book, the first of its kind to be organized in America since Alfred H. Barr Jr.'s pioneering one at the Museum of Modern Art in 1931, has been designed to present as comprehensive a showing of German twentieth-century art as our museum space will permit. It is a qualitative selection, nevertheless, and while all the major German artists of this century are represented, usually by two or more examples of their work, some quite reputable painters and sculptors had to be omitted. This has been done not only for space reasons, but also to avoid the possible tediousness of a survey of more artists than the average gallery visitor is able or willing to digest at one viewing. Fortunately for the reader of this book, both German authors, Dr. Haftmann and Dr. Hentzen, have availed themselves of the opportunity to discuss and to illustrate a number of artists and their works which it was not found possible to include in the exhibition. On other the hand, because of the importance of prints in German twentieth-century art, William S. Lieberman, Curator of Prints, of the Museum of Modern Art, who has been wholly responsible for the print selection in the exhibition, has included and discussed a quite extensive body of graphic work, practically all of it drawn from the Abby Aldrich Rockefeller Print Room of the Museum of Modern Art.

The exhibition begins with the artists of Die Brücke expressionist movement, from its inception about 1905, coincident with the rise of the Fauves in France. It continues through the next wave of German expressionism, known as Der Blaue Reiter, begun in 1911, the Neue Sachlichkeit or New Realism at the end of and immediately after the first World War, the Bauhaus movement of the 1920s and early '30s and, ignoring the false pathos and propaganda art of the Nazi regime, concludes with a highly selective representation of some of the leading artists of post-World War II Germany.

As the one chiefly responsible for the selection of the paintings and sculpture in the exhibition (Dr. Haftmann and Dr. Hentzen have given valuable advice in their respective fields, as has Dr. Kurt Martin, Director of the Fine Arts Academy, Karlsruhe), I have, of course, attempted to secure the finest possible examples of each artist's work; and whatever quality the exhibition possesses is surely due to the extraordinarily generous response of German and American collectors, both public and private, to our requests for loans.

In the preparation of an exhibition as extensive as this one, I have been indebted to many people, not all of whom can be mentioned by name. I wish especially, however, to express my gratitude to the following: The Government of the German Federal Republic for its sponsorship of the exhibition, its grant of funds to cover the costs of shipping and the insuring of all German loans, and its subsidizing of part of the cost of the publication of this book; the Matthew T. Mellon Foundation for a generous grant for this publication; the lenders to the exhibition, whose names appear on page 5; Morton D. May, for his enthusiastic and generous support of the exhibition and book; the directors and curators of American museums, too numerous to list, who graciously advised me of twentieth-century German works in their respective cities; Dr. Bruno Werner, Cultural Counselor to the German Embassy, Washington, D. C., and Dr. Kurt Martin for their great help in working out details of organization; Dr. Leopold Reidemeister, Director of the Wallraf-Richartz Museum, Cologne, and Dr. Will Grohmann for their kindness in introducing me to many private collections in Germany and for their advice in general; for valuable advice in the selection of the exhibition: Dr. W. R. Valentiner, Director, The North Carolina Museum of Art, Raleigh, and Charles L. Kuhn, Curator, Busch-Reisinger Museum of Germanic Culture, Harvard University; for assistance in the preparation of the English text on painting and sculpture: Miss Greta Daniel, Associate Curator of Design, Department of Architecture and Design, Museum of Modern Art; Sam Hunter, Associate Curator of the Department of Painting and Sculpture, and Professor H. W. Janson, Chairman of the Department of Fine Arts, Washington Square College, New York University; Mrs. Gertrud A. Mellon for her exceptional services in the organization of the exhibition; Mrs. Dorothy Simmons and Mrs. Jane Sabersky Isaacson for the index; Miss Frances Pernas, who has seen this book through the press; Charles Oscar, who designed it; and finally, Mrs. Marianne Flack, who has been responsible for the cataloguing of the exhibition and for all the details of correspondence in connection with it.

ANDREW CARNDUFF RITCHIE
Director of the Exhibition

painting

Is there such a thing as a "German" modern art? Is not German merely a geographical term, an historical convention which identifies certain unchangeable and inalienable ways of thought, imagination, and expression with national and language boundaries?

For we all know that one of the most astonishing and significant characteristics of modern man is the really tremendous expansion of his historical and spatial consciousness. The past exists for us in a simultaneous present: the timeless immobility of Egypt, the majesty of ancient Greece, the spiritual magnificence of Byzantium, and the visionary expressiveness of the early peoples of Northern and Western Europe, the precise definition of reality of the Italian Renaissance, the ecstatic illusionism of the Baroque. And this is not all that has gone to shape the consciousness of modern man. He has also heard the voices of the magical cultures of Peru, of Mexico, of pre-Columbian America, and responded to the contemplative poise of the East Asians, the sensuousness of India, and the mysterious sign languages of Africa. All of these cultures have affected us and are a part of modern sensibility.

Similarly there has been a wide expansion of our geographic sense. Modern means of communication, the international scope of commerce, politics, engineering, and transportation, have related the whole world to the individual in his daily life. We may assume that it is an imperative of our time to achieve the spiritual mastery of our expanding global environment and the development of our deepening perspectives of time and space. This global image of the world, arising from practical experience and a new historical consciousness, must be balanced by a corresponding humanitarianism and an adjustment in the emotional life of the individual. It requires a broad human vision which will control the pure thirst for knowledge and prevent it from plunging us into anxiety and despair, as has happened in the realm of modern science.

Art is a fundamental reflection of man's emotional make-up. In fact, the advanced art of our century clearly responded to this new vision of a global culture long before public awareness of it. Suddenly old and remote cultures came alive: the prehistoric, the exotic, the primitive. At the same time the plastic arts of the twentieth century, Fauvism, Cubism, Constructivism, abstract art, Surrealism, were immediately projected upon a supra-national plane, as if all the nations concerned were subject to the same drives and compulsions. Today the impact of Picasso, Klee, and Kandinsky is world-wide.

Modern architecture is the most striking example. Its creative idiom is now international. We must realize the significance of the fact that, for the first time in history, an architect such as Le Corbusier is currently building a city in India (with the open hand as its symbol), and at the same time acting as consultant to city planners in Persia and Colombia, constructing an urban housing development in Marseilles, replanning the city center of St. Dié, and designing buildings for Berlin. It should be noted that Le Corbusier's commissions have not followed in the wake of political conquest, as did those of the architects of the Alexandrian empire, but have been the result rather of a spirit of international cooperation and understanding. Moreover it was in Dessau, an insignificant German town, that the Bauhaus ideas were first developed, ideas of the inter-relationship of the arts which in a short time received international recognition. They have altered our concepts of living space and the design of objects for everyday use.

The importance of the Bauhaus ideas is common knowledge. However there are other impulses originating in Germany which have not received the recognition they deserve. I shall not stress influences of a more personal and ephemeral nature, such as Beckmann's activity in America, or Kirchner's in Switzerland. Let me mention only in passing the great liberating role played by Max Ernst in international Surrealism. More important, it seems to me, has been the particular way in which the German spirit responds to the world and how these responses have affected the sensibilities of other peoples. Paul Klee expressed in his painting and writings one of these facets of the German spirit. He reflected the idea, already implicit in German Romanticism (Novalis, Goethe!), that the visible world of nature is only one manifestation of a much more comprehensive, creative force. Beyond the visible are a multitude of other truths out of which man, from the depths of his being, discovers forms that possess an inner necessity and a natural validity. The Russian Wassily Kandinsky (living however in a German environment) proclaimed another fundamental insight, that creative man is able to report on the world and on life without having to rely on physical appearances. This approach to reality was the essence of abstract painting. Both the above approaches were extraordinarily influential, and radically transformed artistic sensibilities throughout the world. Their spiritual birthplace lay in the northeastern European world of expression, and they could have originated only there. Two other impulses of importance in contemporary art, stemming from the same expressive sources, are found in the work of Hans Hartung and of Wols. Although they both are regarded as members of the École de Paris, they are actually of German origin and are immersed in the northeastern European mode of expression.

At the 1955 international congress of abstract art held in Venice, the well-known Italian artist, Gino Severini, deplored the decline of the Latin spirit of clarity and order caused by the younger painters' addiction to northeastern European Expressionism.

Though stated negatively, this complaint made a positive point. Indeed, we find today a strong international tendency among younger artists towards an abstract Expressionism which releases all their psychic and emotional impulses, a general movement now labeled by such diverse terms as Tachism, Spatialism, and Neo-Expressionism. In time it will be recognized that Wols and Hartung were pioneers of this movement.

Although Germany has made several important contributions toward the development of modern painting, it must be recognized that German artists have not worked in isolation. They could not have achieved what they did unless they had been in contact with the rest of Europe, and particularly with the extraordinarily logical and positive French mind, as represented by an artistic evolution extending from Cézanne, Gauguin, Seurat, van Gogh to Matisse, Picasso, Braque, Delaunay, and Juan Gris.

In speaking of this German contribution, and even of a specific approach of the German mind, I have evidently fallen into a contradiction, having just emphasized the supra-regionalism of modern art. Plastic systems and styles are not isolated things. They have a formal correspondence to a more comprehensive system of relationships in which man of a given period is involved, and into which is tightly woven his attitude to the world and to himself. They are based, therefore, upon a broad human foundation. But this foundation is affected by his surroundings and his origins, by tradition and national peculiarities. We can only understand the interaction of national and international factors in the formation of modern styles if we recognize that modern art is essentially a composite pictorial system to which individuals and regionally determined forces have contributed. Jean Jaurès once expressed poetically a wish which promises to become a reality today: that the peoples of the earth should be like a bouquet of flowers, in which each flower has its own perfume and color, and yet is essential to the effect of the whole bouquet. I believe this concept, which envisages a world-wide federation, exactly illustrates the nature of modern art. And it is a striking fact of our time.

But if this is so, it must be possible to define more precisely those special qualities that give modern German art its individual character within the larger whole.

Characteristics of German Painting

Actually they are not too difficult to define. Since a picture is a visual fact, it is more appropriate to arrive at insight by actual looking than by a discussion of general ideas. Let us therefore compare a few pictures, first a modern French painting and then a modern German painting. As an example, Le Luxe of 1907 by Henri Matisse, representing three female nudes in the open air (page 16). In this classical theme we are immediately struck by the predominance of large uniform color surfaces and decorative, linear

have called the "evocative picture." But, something has been added – and something has been taken away. The picture is remarkably restless and dynamic, pregnant with meaning. We see an expressive space magically illuminated with color and light, in which all poetic transformations seem possible. In this there are imbedded concrete symbols, symbols of animals. These symbols are not accidental; they are integral images taken from nature, which assemble into a typical shape the appearance and essence of the animal. They have a particular job to do in the realm of this picture. They link the abstract organism of the picture to poetic experience that had its origin in nature, and indicate the distance that the creative sensibility of the painter has traveled from its starting point. This "surfacing at another place," as Franz Marc once defined the nature of his artistic activity, removes the accidental and particular experience to a distant poetic sphere, where the general, meaningful, and spiritual qualities within it are realized. A symbol emerges from a fortuitous impulse. Thus this picture is not a harmonious self-sufficient composition; it records the legend of the death and sacrifice of all creatures in nature's hours of destiny, when "the trees display their rings and animals their arteries," as Marc wrote on the back of this painting. Therefore it also possesses the function of illustration. When we compare it with the French picture, it does not aim at the same clear compactness of composition and form; it seems to want to describe other, more comprehensive facts of experience. It is more of an illustration in the higher sense of the term, more a poetic metaphor of universal experience that includes the entire man.

Now for a last comparison, dating from the third decade of the century, in which there began a new geometrization of painting which endeavored to achieve a more universal harmony of measure, number, and proportion. Let us take one of Léger's monumental pictures, the Three Women of 1921 (page 20), which celebrates in a classical theme the experience of the modern workaday world and of technological civilization. We again recognize the formal structure of the "evocative picture" and marvel at the smooth, machine-like precision of form and the stability of the geometrical arrangement of the picture's architecture, the cool, logical exactitude of its intuitive mathematics. When we compare with this picture Schlemmer's Group of Fourteen (page 21), we find a totally different mood, an almost mystical belief in the pictorial significance of the human figure. It is a true image of ideas! Schlemmer attempts, by means of a common spiritual denominator, to harmonize the severe ideality of geometry with the forms of living organic matter. He considers man as the focal point of all material and spiritual, rational, and mystical relationship. He develops a supra-individual, generic symbol – an iconic sign – for the human image as the plastic expression of this belief. This is the fulcrum, the starting point, and center of the composition. Opposed to it there is the dynamic element – space. It is the medium of "internal motion." In this space the figures

Braque: Still Life with Violin and Pitcher. 1909-10. Oil on canvas, $46\,^1/_2 \times 28\,^3/_4''$. Kunstmuseum, Basel, on loan from private collection, Paris (*)

are assigned their places in terms of a formal contest between figure and space that is resolved in a tension-filled design. Here we recognize quite clearly a reflection of Franz Marc's final, highly romantic intention: to give visible expression to what he called the "underlying mystical design of the world," felt and reflected in man.

I think that these comparisons are very instructive. We have seen that the particular modern paintings considered possess similar formal structures and exhibit the same pictorial intentions. For them we have employed such terms as the "evocative surface" and the "evocative picture." We have, therefore, managed to gain an insight, to experience visually the common attributes, the higher relationships, the supra-national element in modern painting. But we have also seen how German paintings exhibit quite specific characteristics within this general structure. We have noted a peculiar restlessness and compression of the new pictorial architecture, which corresponds to a strange deepening of the expressive range, a style of restrained romanticism full of intense adoration of nature and poetic content. The Germans do not conceive of the picture

Marc: Animal Destinies (Tierschicksale). 1913. Oil on canvas, $77^1/_4 \times 104^3/_4''$. Kunstmuseum, Basel (*)

as a self-contained entity, existing only as an object with its autonomous architecture, harmony, order, and form; they also see it as a metaphor of more comprehensive spiritual experiences, as an illustration of man's relation to the universe.

Illustration? That seems to be a derogatory word. But here I agree with the painters themselves. In the summer of 1914 Franz Marc wrote to August Macke, expressly referring to a simular opinion stated by Paul Klee: "I am a German and can only plow my own field; what do I care about the 'peinture' of the French? We Germans are and remain born illustrators even as painters." In fact, we might reduce the difference of formal expression between the French and Germans to this simple pair of concepts: "décor" versus "illustration," provided that we are prepared to restore to these two simple and therefore misused words, "decorative" and "illustrative," their entire spiritual dignity and significance.

General Conditions

These specific characteristics also bear the stamp, of course, of the conditions out of which modern German painting arose. They are quite different, much more complicated and more contradictory than those of French painting. French painting developed with an astonishing consistency. The road from Delacroix and Courbet through Manet to the Impressionists; the subsequent crossings of Impressionist boundary lines of pure optical seeing by Cézanne, Gauguin, van Gogh, and Seurat; the development of a new concept of painting based upon inner vision by the Nabis, Toulouse-Lautrec, and the Neo-Impressionists, and, finally, the resolute conclusions reached by the Fauves and

Léger: Three Women (Le grand déjeuner). 1921.
Oil on canvas, $72\,^1/_4 \times 99''$. The Museum of Modern Art,
New York, Mrs. Simon Guggenheim Fund (*)

Schlemmer: Group of Fourteen in Imaginary Architecture·
1930. Oil and tempera on canvas, $35^{7}/_{8} \times 47^{1}/_{4}''$.
Wallraf-Richartz Museum, Cologne (*)

the Cubists – all of this displays a remarkable, faultless logic. One developed out of
the other and called forth the third in small, coherent steps. None of this is to be found
in Germany; here the situation is strangely blurred and disjointed at the beginning of
the century. We need not think of the painters who stood in the forefront of fashionable
taste during the Kaiser Wilhelm boom years and masked the true artistic developments –
the military, historical, and portrait painters of the era, such as Anton von Werner,
Piloty, Defregger, and Lenbach – for France also had its share of such traditionalists
in its Meissoniers and Bouguereaus. This picture is very contradictory even in the
higher ranks of art. On the one hand, we have the aristocratic idealism of Hans von
Marées, who stems from the great draftsmen of the Italian Renaissance and formulates
his doctrine of the inward concept of images taken from visible nature but developed
from pure perception, which is so strangely parallel to the thinking of Cézanne. Just
before the turn of the century Marées was accorded the recognition that was denied
him during his lifetime (he died in Rome in 1887), mainly as the result of the clear
interpretation of his plastic thought by Konrad Fiedler, and the theoretical work of the
sculptor Adolf von Hildebrand. What continued to live in his ideas was this extension
and clarification of pure perception by the inner imagination, and the emphasis upon
design and form. "The Problem of Form" was the title of the well-known book by Adolf
von Hildebrand, which was based upon the ideas of Marées. On the other hand, there
was Böcklin's world of highly romantic images. This not only contained a new mythology

of the romantic German feeling for nature, and transformed a new spirituality of nature into figurative allegories, but also charged composition and form with new content. The architecture of the picture was put to the service of nature poetry, and color was intensified to a richness of expression uncommon in the past. Klinger and Franz von Stuck adopted this manner of painting. Von Stuck combined it with the concept of the Jugendstil, provided a forum for it in the Munich Secession founded in 1893, and transmitted it to the younger generation in his work as a teacher in the Munich Academy after 1895. Such important figures as Klee and Kandinsky were pupils of Stuck.

Opposed to this high-strung romantic idealism was a quiet, simple mode of nature painting whose master was Wilhelm Leibl. And this naturalistic tendency similarly split into two distinct movements which were also geographically separated. One had as its champion Max Liebermann, with its center of action the Berlin Secession founded in 1892, and as its background the new metropolitan society of Berlin whose esthetic views were sharply opposed to the imperial court and its representational arts that extolled the military and the empire. The new, unassuming, and personal nature-painting was the artistic reflection of the democratic and liberal ideas of these circles, and comprised German Impressionism. It entered into contact with French Impressionism at an early date, to be sure, but it was also based upon a provincial development of its own in the paintings of Menzel. Its immediate source was not in France, but in the Netherlands, in Dutch plein-air painting, as developed by Jongkind (who in turn was stimulated by the Barbizon school), and by Israel. This rather Nordic origin left a very characteristic mark upon German Impressionism, in the remarkable preference for poetic figure groups and in a lyrical concept of nature. The two strongest powers contributing to Berlin Impressionism at the beginning of the century, Slevogt and Corinth, had begun originally with romantic figure painting.

The romanticism that affected German art found eloquent expression in highly poetic landscape painting that intensified a feeling for nature and an exalted human mood, painting that must really be called German nature lyricism. Curiously corresponding to the Pont-Aven circle of painters inspired by Gauguin, and to the Breton and Scottish landscape schools, groups of painters formed artist colonies in North and South Germany and tried to capture the spirit of unspectacular nature in their paintings of out-of-the-way, unspoiled villages, heaths, and marshes. As far back as 1890 a group of painters came together in the small village of Worpswede, in North Germany, and soon thereafter arose the school of Dachau in southern Germany. By 1895 the Worpswede painters had already captured the gold medals in the Munich Crystal Palace exhibition, thus attaining official recognition. German nature lyricism was of considerable importance in the rise of German Expressionism. Nolde, Rohlfs, and Paula Modersohn-Becker grew out of it directly. As a matter of fact, here we find the germs of an Expressionist interpretation of nature, and of the things and forces within it. In the violet pools of water in the marshes, in the blaze of the evening sun, with the large simple silhouettes of houses and trees against the glowing heavens, in the simple gestures of people who worked the soil, there lay a great temptation to express the primitive essence of this nature and its quality of myth by heightening and simplifying forms and colors. Only the shadows of the old romantic tradition still obscured the expressive possibilities latent in the pictorial means themselves, in line, form, and color.

But now an attitude penetrated into this complex milieu from the unexpected direction of the applied arts, meeting these latent possibilities of expression more than halfway. This was the Jugendstil. It derived its name from the magazine Jugend, founded in Munich in 1896, which became the spokesman of the new movement, together with the satirical magazine Simplizissimus founded at the same time, and Pan which Meier-Graefe first published in 1895. The movement had broad international connections. It was allied to the English arts and crafts movement initiated by Morris and Ruskin, whose magazine The Studio, founded in 1893 and widely distributed in Germany, had become the vehicle of the English ideas. But the Jugendstil was also closely connected with the Belgian and Scottish applied-arts movements and with French Art Nouveau. Hence before French Impressionism itself had really taken root in Germany, the bold ideas that supplanted it were already at work in the German milieu. They were the ideas of the French Nabis, whose organ of publication was La Revue Blanche, founded in 1891. Bonnard, Vuillard, Denis, and Sérusier, with their flat décor and artificially simple "gaucherie," were important influences. In the case of Sérusier and Maurice Denis these influences were early associated with a romantic religious revival which rapidly came into contact with a similar trend in Germany in the school of monastic painting of Kloster Beuron and Father Desiderius Lenz. Then there was Toulouse-Lautrec; but above all there was French Neo-Impressionism. In the very late works of Seurat, such as Le Chahut of 1890, a new organization of the picture surface had been developed. An expressive, undulating arabesque gathered the defining contours of objects into its rhythmic flow, and over the surface, consisting of tiny dots of pure pigment, spread a curiously magical radiance of color. Paul Signac had picked up these suggestions of Seurat, and from them developed a highly decorative style of painting which often reached the phantasmagorical in color expression. He based his style upon a theory that emphasized the constructive and expressive possibilities of the pure pictorial means. His book "From Delacroix to Neo-Impressionism" appeared in German translation in 1899, after Germany had already seen exhibitions of his work. This book contained revolutionary statements: "Art as creation is superior to the copying of nature." An entirely new concept of painting was set forth: "Facing his blank canvas, the painter should above all decide which lines and surface effects, which colors and tones are to cover it . . . He

Caricature from Simplicissimus. 1896 (*)

plays with the range of his colors . . . Surrendering completely to the pleasure of controlling the play and struggle of the seven prismatic colors, he is like a musician who varies the seven notes of the scale. He will adapt line, chiaroscuro, and color to the character he wants the picture to have. By subordinating color and line to the emotion he feels, the painter becomes a poet, a creator." These were the ideas that had so profound an effect in the German milieu.

A satirical drawing (above) dating from 1896 provides an insight into a German studio of the time better than any words can do. The figure of the artist, which typifies the "modern" artist of that period, is shown with a gay candor. He is the dandy type, the peculiar artistic stylization of the English gentleman that Walter Pater had sketched, and Oscar Wilde had personified for the entire decade, though strangely blended with the French "decadent" typical of the French Symbolist movement, and all in a cloud of German "profundity," of course. We can easily imagine the literary texts from which this painter had formulated his attitude to life: doubtless from Oscar Wilde, but also from Baudelaire, from Strindberg and, of course, from Nietzsche. (The very first issue of Pan in 1895 begins with Nietzsche's "Zarathustra before the King.") The paintings represented in this drawing are as complex as the artist himself. In the representation of Salome with the head of John, and in the shrieking Medusa head, we see the studiously literary, demonic quality of Stuck. The picture of the snake, dagger, and lily, and the portrait of a woman elaborately framed by linear decoration and doubtlessly called Sphinx, show the fascination with allegory and the ornamental line of the Jugendstil. On the easel at the right we find a motif that is especially treasured by the school of German nature lyricism, Girl Playing a Flute in a Spring Landscape. In the background there is a seascape which belongs to the stock of motifs of the Impressionist plein-air group; and in the foreground there is a picture whose Pointillist manner confirms for us the influence of Neo-Impressionism. Thus we see how many diverse tendencies of a human, literary, and formal nature made their way into a German painter's studio of the time! But there is something they all had in common: the effort to elevate painting to a poetic level where the significance of pure color and of expressive arabesque are fully realized.

In fact, the Jugendstil already carried within it an awareness of the expressive possibilities of the pictorial means themselves, and that awareness eventually and logically led to abstract painting. The very concept of "abstract style" arose shortly before 1900, as a term to designate an ornamental manner developed from non-objective arabesques, and it is opposed to the "floral style" which represented flowers, tendrils, and creepers. The spokesman for the abstract style was the Belgian, Henri van de Velde, who propagated in Germany toward the end of the century the ideas of Art Nouveau and of Neo-Impressionism developed in Paris. He insisted upon abstract style because it seemed to him that the natural form merely blurred the expressive power of the pictorial means. "A line," he taught, "is a force; it derives its force from the energy of the man who drew it."

This agreed with the ideas circulating in Germany. The apostle of Jugendstil, Hermann Bahr, preached the "music of colors" and looked for a public "that no longer demands any object, but is happy to listen to the music of colors." The painter and architect Endell wrote of "the power of pure colors over the human mind"; the sculptor Obrist talked of the psychic power of abstract forms; and the psychologist Theodor Lipps delivered lectures at the University of Munich on the psychic effect of "organized lines," lectures which enjoyed considerable repute among artists. All of this prior to and around 1900! Endell did a giant relief in free abstract forms on the façade of the Elvira Photo Studio in Munich, while Obrist designed embroidery and called one of these largely abstract designs Crack of the Whip. His decorative designs for fountains could be regarded, no doubt, as early forms of abstract sculpture. It is from suggestions such as these that the painter Hölzel was stimulated to explore the laws which govern purely pictorial means and to investigate their capacity to express the spiritual element in art. In the guise of ornamental forms, the first unfaltering steps were taken toward the complete abandonment of pictures derived from the actual phenomena of nature. A number of artists turned to abstract symbols which were drawn from the more arbitrary expressive tendencies of a nature lyricism and to the abstract-constructive arrangement of colors found in Neo-Impressionism. A distant objective flashed into view: by continuously spiritualizing, charging, and condensing the ornamental and the decorative, it became possible to build a bridge from applied art to a new free domain in which art itself became an expressive movement, the reproduction and evocation of spiritual stimuli in an allegory of free color forms. Although these German experiments did not produce a pictorial genius, we must not overlook the extraordinary perspective they set forth. They led straight from the abstract style of the Jugendstil and the arguments associated with it to the abstract painting of Kandinsky, which was born directly out of this climate.

And now the encouraging example of great individuals began to take effect in this pregnant milieu. First there was the Norwegian Edvard Munch, who had had his first big show in Berlin as far back as 1892, and to whom a group of leading poets and writers on art in Berlin had dedicated a book as early as 1895. Actually Munch was a painter who was able to turn all the aspirations of the decade into pictures in which the myth of the world of Nordic destiny was embodied in a completely new, bold manner of giving expressive value to forms and colors. Then there was the Swiss, Ferdinand Hodler, whose broad ornamental approach and emotion-charged, rhythmic organization of the canvas by gestural and formal repetition appealed so strongly to German artists. And now the French began to be more and more influential: first the late Impressionists, and especially Monet, whose shimmering color this German milieu could reinterpret in terms of the fabulous and phantasmagoric just as they did with the open color designs of the Neo-Impressionists. And soon there appeared the great revolutionaries, Gauguin and van Gogh; Cézanne significantly remained in the background even though the Berlin National Gallery under Hugo von Tschudi had acquired a painting by him as early as 1899. This entire structure was supported, and provided with spiritual underpinning, mainly by a select group of museum curators, writers on art, collectors and art teachers, such as Hugo von Tschudi, Count Harry Kessler, Julius Meier-Graefe, Alfred Lichtwarck, Ernst Osthaus, and Henri van de Velde. And it is this group of sensitive spirits that began to trace the sources of man's first and most primitive expression. Here, then, are the origins of the preoccupation with the early forms of art, with the mode of expression of primitive peoples, with folk art, and the drawings of children. Here again we find a sign post, pointing to a new goal.

This cursory summary would not be complete, however, if we did not at least call attention to the general spiritual background and framework of these developments. For the German "fin-de-siècle" was in a state of powerful spiritual fermentation which was undermining all the barriers of tradition and convention. Wagner's mythic symbolism had already produced an excited response. Now the visionary ideas of the Rosicrucians and the obscure verbal splendor and subtle sensibility of the French Symbolists flooded in from the West. And from the North, with Ibsen, Strindberg and Jacobsen, there came a new, complicated psychological view of man, displaying the many facets of his personality, his enigmatic nature, and the extent to which he was at the mercy of the stirrings of the soul. The verbal brilliance and the intellectual magic of Friedrich Nietzsche broke upon this restlessness like a bombshell. His aristocratic, anti-bourgeois attitude, his desperate struggle for a new vision of man, his insistence upon the dignity and the inalienable individuality of the self, his lofty and gigantic perspectives of a revolutionary transvaluation created a wholly new point of departure. This outlook contained nothing precise, philosophical, or theoretical; it was a revolution in mental attitude, a spirit of critical and creative freedom which acknowledged no tradition, and obeyed itself alone with joyous aggressiveness. The new mood gave way to what was probably one of the most remarkable phenomena in modern history, the German youth movement, in which an entire generation prepared, under the slogan "war against school and home," to reshape their lives and to attain a new approach to nature, to reality, and to the community of man.

It was this unusually complex situation that was the breeding ground for the new art movements of the twentieth century in Germany. On careful reflection, we find that out of this background the spiritual attitude of Expressionism follows with the inner consistency that is always the mark of genuine spiritual events.

Origin of Expressionism

We may take the years 1905-06 as the key period for the birth of German Expressionism. 1905 is the year in which the Fauves appeared as a group in the Paris Autumn Salon. The extension of the human situation made the problem for painting quite clear. The allegorical cloak that obscured the vision of reality had to be pushed aside, a new dialogue with the world had to be initiated, unburdened by tradition and history, and this direct relationship between nature and the ego had to be expressed with as much force as possible. The center of gravity no longer lay in things themselves, but in the sensation they produced, for which a new language now had to be found. It was only natural that the painters sought out the intimations of this direct language where they did: in the art of primitive peoples, in peasant folklore, in the forms created by the "naive," and by children.

German Expressionism arose simultaneously in artists' associations geographically separated and working independently of each other: the Brücke in Dresden, the Neue Künstler-Vereinigung in Munich, from which the Blaue Reiter seceded, and in the work of individuals. Only around 1910 and 1911 did it coalesce into a general stylistic expression.In North Germany it was brought about by the work of three important individuals who had no contact with one another: Paula Modersohn-Becker, Christian Rohlfs, and Emil Nolde.

Modersohn-Becker: Self Portrait with Camellia. 1907.
Oil on board, $23\,^5/_8 \times 11''$. Folkwang Museum, Essen

Modersohn-Becker: Old Peasant Woman. 1906-07. Oil on canvas, $30^1/_4 \times 22^1/_2''$. Private collection, U.S.A.

Paula Modersohn-Becker (1876-1907) came directly from the school of German nature lyricism. She had moved to Worpswede in 1899, had worked with Mackensen, and had married the Worpswede painter Modersohn in 1901. Her friendship with Rilke and Carl Hauptmann put this highly emotional young woman in contact with the spiritual stimuli that were agitating Europe. In 1900 she was in Paris and discovered for herself Millet and the Breton landscape painters; in other words, she saw French painting through Worpswede eyes. But as early as 1903 she was back in Paris in order "to regard Worpswede through a critical lens." The nature lyricism of the Worpswede school had already become too genre-like for her. She sought a "great simplicity of form" which should aim at and strike to the simple core of things and convey the gripping emotion ignited by this new reality. She then began to see the things and people around her as "great in their simplicity." She reduced each objective form to its essential formal rudiments, thus obtaining an expressive pictorial vocabulary with which objects and the sensations they occasion could be described "as with runic writing." What happened, she felt, was that in looking at the fragmented multiplicity of nature, one's sensibilities became confused, and she as a painter had to refer to the poetic counterpart for experience in her imagination: "One should not think so much about nature when painting a picture. Make the color sketch approximately as you felt it in nature." In this concentrated labor, essentially very lonely, a manner of handling form grew up slowly within her that enabled her to understand immediately the vision of Gauguin and Cézanne when she encountered their works in Paris in 1905 and 1906. Death prevented Paula Modersohn-Becker from building upon this fortunate encounter a rich body of work, and one of her last wishes was to be able to travel to Paris again, because "fifty-six Cézanne's were being

Rohlfs: Dark Mountains. 1912. Oil on canvas, $31^7/_8 \times 39^1/_2''$. Kleemann Galleries, New York

Rohlfs: Amazon. 1912. Oil on canvas, $31\,^1/_2 \times 39\,^3/_8''$. Folkwang Museum, Essen

shown." Thus her work remained a fragment. But in her portraits (page 79) the expressive definition of form, whose essential core also revealed the universal, mythic center of the human being portrayed, and the ceremonially rigorous style of her self portraits which are invested with the highly emotional humanity of this young woman (Self Portrait with Camellia, page 28), indicate the distance that already separated her from Worpswede nature lyricism.

Paula Modersohn-Becker had crossed the threshold to the art of expression in a completely independent, almost compulsive evolution. And this same necessity is exhibited in the work of Christian Rohlfs (1849-1938). Rohlfs was fifty-six years old when he found his own Expressionist style. He had begun as a landscape painter in Weimar and in constant development had traveled from an intimate naturalism to a reserved Impressionism. In the circle of van de Velde, who had taken over the direction of the Applied Arts School in Weimar at the beginning of the century, he encountered the late Impressionism of Monet, Neo-Impressionism, and shortly thereafter, van Gogh. Then Osthaus, who was at the time building up his collection of these French innovators, took him along to Hagen. In Osthaus' extremely European environment the nearly sixty-year-old Rohlfs went through a stormy period of growth. The tremulous light – intensified to the point of incorporeality – radiated by the color of the late Monet, the dramatic power of color and the free handling of the pictorial means displayed by van Gogh were the problems to be solved. His goal was a new Expressionist lyricism. From these points of departure, Rohlfs succeeded in arriving at his initial solutions in Soest in the summer months of 1905-06. They are views of this medieval town, architectural paintings in pure luminous color like the cathedrals of Monet but executed in a spontaneous script whose calligraghy points to van Gogh. The subject matter was resolutely fused with the picture surface and the color ornamentally arranged in strong, pure tones. The picture acquires the character of a colored window, illuminated from within. Having reached this point, Rohlfs in his further development was concerned with making the individual elements grow together, in order to reinforce the scintillation and the hovering quality of the incorporeal color. Color is simplified to red-blue-yellow, a dominant fundamental, and a rising accompanying tone attuned to it. The basic colors are made to vibrate by constant transitions and crossings. The oscillation of the surface dematerializes the motif, and the lyrical and legendary discovered within it appear on the evocative surface. The picture becomes a visual poem.

For this pictorial transformation always involved a new way of perceiving reality. It sought the profound, the primeval, the legend woven into nature. It was this new perception that led Rohlfs to find in late French Impressionism the new means required for the desired intensification of the expressive content of painting – a highly creative misunderstanding. This same key word, misunderstanding, also applies (in the period

Nolde: Christ Among the Children. 1910. Oil on canvas, $34^1/_8 \times 41^7/_8''$. The Museum of Modern Art, gift of Dr. W. R. Valentiner

1905-06) to the third of the North German Expressionists, Emil Nolde, when, at the age of forty, he saw for the first time works by the Frenchmen Monet, Gauguin, and van Gogh, in the circle of Osthaus.

Emil Nolde (1867-1956) had been exposed to Dachau nature lyricism in 1898, and in Paris in 1900 to the paintings of Manet, Daumier, and Goya. Stimulated by these influences, he sought to translate into pictorial terms the chthonian, mythic, and legendary forces which he saw all about him in nature. When he saw the new French paintings he broke out of the tonality of the Munich school and the lyricism of the Dachau group into a world of free, luminous color. Thus he substituted the sensuous, symbolic power of color for the literary and the metaphorical. He had scarcely encountered late Impressionism when he began an ecstatic reinterpretation of it. He painted landscapes, pictures of gardens and flowers whose violent color and spontaneous calligraphy raised the motif wholly beyond the representational, earning him in 1906 the invitation of the Brücke painters to join their association as "payment for these storms of color." But Nolde's chthonian concept of nature and his fantasy which sought the mythical were much too personal to be able to ripen in a community. He had other companions – van Gogh, Munch, Ensor. He was opposed to discussion, opposed to intellect, in favor of the pure painterly instinct, for which a "vague notion only in glow and color" sufficed as the impulse for a painting. In 1909 he tried to come closer to the mythical in religious paintings: he painted a Pentecost and the Last Supper and let this series culminate in the altar-like iconostasis of the 1911 cycle of the life of Christ. These are paintings of powerful expressiveness in which typified masks and archaic gestures evoke faces of barbaric power, and the glow of the color shifts the setting into the legendary and the other-worldly. This brought him close to the elemental powers of the art of primitive people. In 1913-14 Nolde went to New Guinea. What he described in his diary there as characteristic of primitive art also defines the core of his own art: "the absolute originality, the intensive, often grotesque expression of force and life in the simplest form." Here we see Nolde's recurring fundamental experience, experiencing nature as a mythical encounter. It is this expressive feeling for nature that makes him do battle with Liebermann's Impressionism and the Berlin Secession, and makes his generation regard him as the champion of a new German art. His fantasy is always located in those human zones where the myth arises out of ancient memories. The close-up view of things, the simple, archaic power of the composition, the blazing allegorical value of color are the means employed to present this mythicalism on the canvas. In the 'twenties the landscape becomes more prominent. The dramatic is transformed into the epic. Nature becomes a luminous legend. The experiencing of reality, which had appeared under the aspect of an intimate expressive relationship between the world and man at the beginning of the century, had now found a mode of expression.

Nolde: Three Russians. 1915. Oil on burlap, 28 $^3/_4$ × 39 $^1/_2$″. Collection Richard L. Feigen, New York

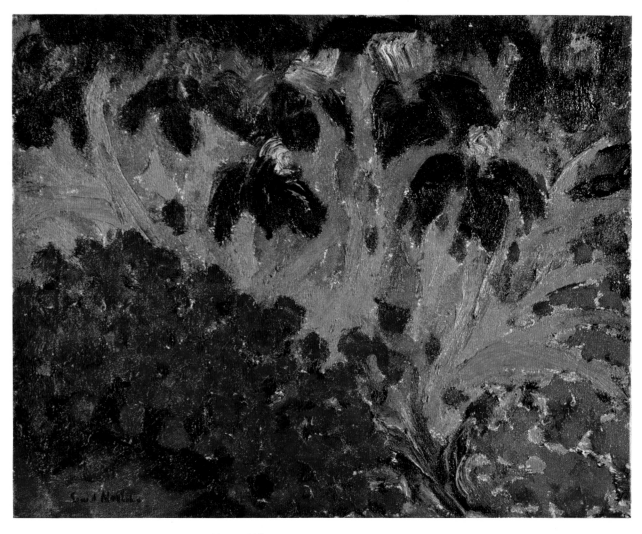

Nolde: Flowers. c. 1915? Oil on burlap, $26\,^1/_4 \times 33\,^1/_4''$. The Museum of Modern Art, New York, gift of Mr. and Mrs. Werner E. Josten

above, Nolde: Stormy Landscape. c. 1920? Oil on canvas, 29 × 39³/₄″. Staatliche Kunsthalle, Karlsruhe

Nolde: Amaryllis and Anemone. Watercolor, 13³/₄ × 18³/₈″. The Museum of Modern Art, New York, gift of Philip L. Goodwin

The Brücke Community of Artists

While this new spirit operated within the individual in North Germany, in Central Germany it brought together in a community a group of very young artists for whom this very community and camaraderie provided a fresh spirit of aggressiveness. In 1904 four young student painters of the Dresden Institute of Technology came to know each other: Kirchner, Heckel, Schmidt-Rottluff, and Bleyel, and in 1905 they founded an artist's association which they called Die Brücke (The Bridge). Their collective studio was an empty shoemaker's store. Here a joint style was evolved out of a feeling of spiritual solidarity, and they lived the dream of communion which van Gogh and Gauguin had dreamed before them.

The Brücke had no program. In 1906 Kirchner did a small manifesto in the form of a woodcut which, together with a general appeal to youth, contained nothing but the assertion that everyone "who portrays, directly, without qualification, the creative impulse" belongs to the Brücke. In a letter of 1906, in which Schmidt-Rottluff asked Nolde to join them, he also stated as the objective of the Brücke merely "the attraction of young and fermenting elements."

Light is shed upon the inner state of these young painters by a report made by Kirchner on Heckel's first visit to him, the latter climbing the studio staircase with a shirt open at the collar, with provocatory poetic flourish, and declaiming "Zarathustra" aloud. This feverish consciousness of being of an elite characterizes the Brücke community, which had chosen as its motto Horace's "Odi profanum vulgus." It nourished itself on the reading of Verlaine, Rimbaud, D'Annunzio, Jacobsen, Walt Whitman, Dostoyevsky, Strindberg, Wedekind, Hölderlin, and, over and over again, Nietzsche.

The Brücke held its first exhibition in 1906 in the showroom of a Dresden lamp factory; this was followed in 1907 by a second show in Richter's art gallery, in which Pechstein and Nolde, who had been recruited in 1906, also participated. The two shows achieved nothing but a "succès de scandale" which accompanied the Brücke artists for a long time.

What was shown in these exhibitions was painting of great spontaneity, motifs taken directly from nature, landscapes, nudes, but presented in a summary, hasty symbolic script and in shouting, luminous color which tended to accumulate in large color areas despite the rapidity of the brush work. Spontaneous and personal as this early Brücke idiom may have appeared – and doubtless was – the sources that came together there, releasing a style of great homogeneity, were very diverse. To be sure the burning spirit of van Gogh was already at work; the young painters were also aware of the Impressionist means and the Neo-Impressionist theory of the division of color into its pure values, which Kirchner had been able to study in an exhibition organized by Kandinsky

Kirchner: Dodo and Her Brother. 1905-06.
Oil on canvas, $67\,^1/_4 \times 37\,^1/_2''$. Smith College
Museum of Art, Northampton, Massachusetts

Kirchner: Zurich. 1926. Oil on canvas, 53 × 47″. Collection Mr. and Mrs. Bruce B. Dayton, Minneapolis

opposite, Kirchner: The Painters of the Brücke. 1925.
Oil on canvas, 66 1/8 × 49 5/8″. Wallraf-Richartz Museum, Cologne

It is shown too in Kirchner's street scene by the hectic figurative symbols, the restless interlacing of the space, and the desperate tension of color, all of which superlatively reflect the spiritual and historical situation – Berlin's Kurfürstendamm in 1913!

It was only natural that the varied individualities involved in this new, highly expressive style, a style which encouraged self-revelation, should grow apart. This brought the community to an end. The Brücke collapsed in 1913.

The intimate community of the Brücke artists in which fundamental formal, technical, or pictorial discoveries were immediately seized upon by the entire group enable us to trace the development of Brücke Expressionism as a collective movement. If we were to characterize the different personalities more precisely, we might say that Kirchner was the richest in ideas, the most sensitive, and the most gifted, always insisting on imposing his own intensified, feverish mood upon the picture; that Heckel was the lyricist who sought to report his poetic experiences; and that Schmidt-Rottluff was closest to the earth, full of power, and most in need of putting his experience of nature in monumental form. Otto Mueller, more at the periphery of the Brücke, was the gentle poet who throughout his life dreamed a simple Arcadian dream. But all these personalities fitted smoothly into a common style of expression.

At the break-up of the community the various members parted company and went their own ways. Erich Heckel (born 1883) turned slowly to a more lyrical concept of nature, thought he did not break entirely with the stylistic program of the Brücke. The same is true of Karl Schmidt-Rottluff (born 1884), and of Otto Mueller (1874-1930) who arrived at a simple, monumental, and brilliantly colored vision of nature. Note especially Mueller's landscapes, his figures on the shores of lakes, his nude, sharp-breasted gypsies, their huts silhouetted against the dark glory of colored planes, a sunflower looking like a melancholy star – the vision gradually reaching a mythical radiance.

Ernst Ludwig Kirchner (1880-1938) who became a patient in Davos, Switzerland in 1917 experienced the broadest development. This man of the big city comes face to face in Switzerland with the austere mountain scenery and seeks and finds a large-scale, runic script of epic character. He now records his new experience of reality in these hieroglyphs that denote objects. His mountain landscapes and simple monumental pictures are taken from the life of the peasants. Their structure is very severe, emphasizing a framework of verticals and horizontals. The pictures now assume the monumental character of tapestries (page 45). Soon after 1928 Kirchner's style changes again; Picasso begins to affect it. His cursive writings now reach into more abstract regions. Simultaneity of front and side views, the tying of separate objective forms into a single arabesque, rhythmic mirrorings, the separation of unified complex forms by color; by all these devices the picture is transformed into an abstract, rhythmic-ornamental structure. Shortly before his death Kirchner seemed about to enter a new creative

Heckel: Two Men at a Table. 1912. Oil on canvas, $38\,^1/_4 \times 47\,^1/_4''$. Kunsthalle, Hamburg

Heckel: A Crystal Day. 1913. Oil on canvas, $47\,^1/_4 \times 37\,^3/_4''$. Collection Max Kruss, Berlin

Schmidt-Rottluff: Rising Moon. 1912. Oil on canvas, 34 $\frac{1}{2}$ × 37 $\frac{1}{2}$″. Collection Mr. and Mrs. Morton D. May, St. Louis, Missouri

Schmidt-Rottluff: Pharisees. 1912. Oil on canvas, $29^7/_8 \times 40^1/_2''$. The Museum of Modern Art, New York, Mrs. Gertrud A. Mellon Fund

opposite, Schmidt-Rottluff: Washerwomen by the Sea. 1921. Oil on canvas, $38^1/_2 \times 44''$. Collection Mr. and Mrs. Richard K. Weil, St. Louis, Missouri

cycle. His latest pictures reproduced nature in a less altered form. But Kirchner had no more time left to him. Terrified by the symptoms of his recurrent illness, despondent over the iconoclasm of a Germany rapidly turning barbarian, which confiscated, mocked, and destroyed his works, the painter, whose heart's desire was the renewal of German art, committed suicide on June 15, 1938.

If we are to summarize the achievements of the Brücke, we might say that it succeeded in finding a language for a fundamental transformation of the experience of reality, by which the new perception of reality could be expressed. It was an insight into the representational independence of the pictorial means, whereby line, form, color, space, became self-sufficient entities and conveyed expression beyond the literary; and

Mueller: Three Girls in the Woods. c. 1920. Oil on burlap, 48 × 53″. Collection Mr. and Mrs. Morton D. May, St. Louis, Missouri

Mueller: A Pair of Lovers. c. 1928. Oil on board, $39\,^3/_8 \times 29\,^7/_8''$. Dr. Bernhard Sprengel, Hanover

it was finally the slow elaboration of the visual field, upon which the new contact with reality could be deposited as a picture, the evocative surface. Only upon such a surface, which held nothing visible in the sense of an imitative realism but merely evoked a relationship to reality, could the actual experience of reality be recorded in runic writing or in hieroglyphs. It is this achievement in the pictorial that gives the Brücke its spiritual importance and, at the same time, relates it more closely to the phalanx of Frenchmen, led by the genius of Matisse and the Fauves.

The Blaue Reiter

While the Brücke were active in North and Central Germany, a small circle of painters had gathered in Munich around the Russian Wassily Kandinsky. Kandinsky had entered the Jugendstil milieu of Munich in 1896; he had studied with Stuck and had learned how to express his Russian fantasy of fairy tale and legend in the language of the Munich Jugendstil. After 1903 other travels took him to Italy, Tunisia, and often to France, acquainting him with the new color of the Neo-Impressionists and the Fauves. But all this was linked up for him with old recollections of vivid Russian folklore, which he now encountered again in the peasant art of Upper Bavaria, forcing him to seek the possibilities of spontaneous, naive, spiritual expression behind the decorative and constructive – the artistic values of color. At an early date he was joined by another Russian, Alexei von Jawlensky, who had encountered the painting of Cézanne, van Gogh, and Matisse in Paris, and now tried to intensify the new, skillfully managed color of the French into the transcendental, in his own Russian manner. Their two friends, Gabrielle Münter and Marianne von Werefkin, and a few other painters enlarged the loose association, and out of it there arose in 1909 the New Artists Association of Munich. In addition to those mentioned above, its members included Erbslöh, Kanoldt, and Kubin. In 1910 Bechtejeff, Karl Hofer, Moissey, Kogan, and Pierre Girieud were added. An initial exhibition was held in the winter of 1909; another in the autumn of 1910, in which the young painters of the French avant garde were also represented: Picasso, Braque, Derain, van Dongen, Rouault, and Vlaminck. What was shown was the Fauvism of Kandinsky and Jawlensky, raised to the level of spontaneous and naive expression, and the work of Erbslöh and Kanoldt, inspired by the Jugendstil. The pictorial credo of the group of painters can be perfectly summarized in the words of Otto Fischer in his book "Das Neue Bild" of 1912, dedicated to the New Artists Association: "Color is a means of expression that speaks directly to the soul. It is not correct drawing that portrays the nature of things, but rather the spirited and expressive contour. Things are not things alone if they are the expression of the soul."

But Kandinsky was involved in stormy intellectual developments during 1910 and

Marc: Fighting Cows. 1911. Oil on canvas, $32\,^3/_4 \times 54''$. Private collection, New York

1911 which extended far beyond the boundaries of the New Artists Association and attracted new, unusually talented painters. Franz Marc, August Macke, and soon Paul Klee joined him in 1911. In 1910 Kandinsky had summarized his ideas in a manuscript of a book, "The Spiritual in Art" (published in 1912). This is a polemic against materialism and calls for a new spiritualization of life. Just as science had dissolved substance and matter, just as Matisse and Picasso had prepared a new spiritual view of the objective world, all painting must now be liberated from its function of reproducing the world of material objects and become a spiritual evocation and activity. The culminating idea of the book is the statement: "The harmony of color and form must be based solely upon the principle of the proper contact with the human soul." The music of abstract color areas should be sufficient to carry the inner music of things, to which man's soul responds. Thinking along these lines, Kandinsky in 1910 had already painted, in bold

Marc: Blue Horses. 1911. Oil on canvas, 41 $^3/_8$ × 71 $^3/_8$". Walker Art Center, Minneapolis, Minnesota

anticipation, his first abstract picture. These were the ideas that so greatly excited his friends, and which they associated with their own romantic, religious conviction of a great existential bond linking man and the universe, for which the painter, using new tools, could erect pictorial allegories, "symbols that belong on the altars of the coming spiritual religion," as Franz Marc put it.

But these ideas were far beyond the comprehension of many of the other artists in the New Artists Association. As a result the association broke up in December 1911. On December 18, 1911 the circle around Kandinsky and Marc opened an exhibition of its own under the title Der Blaue Reiter in which Kandinsky, Marc, Macke, Campendonk, the Burliuk brothers, the musician Arnold Schönberg, and the Frenchman Delaunay (as an example of the "great abstract" tendency), and Henri Rousseau (as an example of the "great real" tendency) took part. A graphic show was held in the Goltz art gallery in March 1912; it included, in addition to the Blaue Reiter group, Kubin and Klee, the Frenchmen Braque, Derain, de la Fresnaye, Picasso, and Vlaminck, the painters of the Brücke, Hans Arp, and the Russians Larionoff, Gontcharova, and Malevich.

Exhibitions were held in Cologne, Berlin, Hagen, and Frankfurt. In 1913 the Blaue Reiter again exhibited as a group in Herwarth Walden's Berlin Autumn Salon. Then the war tore the group apart.

The solid core of the Blaue Reiter consisted of Kandinsky, Marc, Macke, Jawlensky, and Klee. The name was taken from a book that Kandinsky and Marc edited in 1911 and published in 1912. This dealt with the works of the naive artist: peasant glass painting, old German woodcuts, and children's drawings. It described the new anti-naturalist movements in Germany, Russia, and France. Schönberg wrote on the corresponding developments in music. Kandinsky developed his ideas and contributed a play "Der gelbe Klang" ("The Yellow Sound"). An intense frame of mind prevails throughout this beautiful volume, a spirit close to those great spiritual objectives that Franz Marc had defined in a romantic, paradoxical, but unusually significant formulation as, "sensing the underlying mystical design of the visible world."

What Franz Marc (1880-1916) meant by that can be seen in his pictures. Their great theme is animals, for, in Marc's vision, the entire life and being of animals seemed to be part of an existing natural order. If one could penetrate the animal spirit, and enrich one's visual imagination with images stemming from the deeper knowledge of the nature of animals, it would be possible to return to this order, the Franciscan "ordo caritatis," and to take from it more unified images. For visible nature is only one point of departure. And thus in the Red Horses or in the famous Tower of Blue Horses (page 58) we see the symbol of the animal appear in radiant red or blue, because the expression demands such spiritual resplendence. In the Tower of Blue Horses, a motif that Marc saw in the pastures of Lenggries, he erects a transparent architecture of animal bodies. Their refulgent blues become a spiritual link to the sign of heaven, a cathedral of creature forms in the great sweep of the world. Animal Destinies (page 19) tells us of the death and sacrifice of animals; their place and participation in the great chorus of being is the theme of the painting, Deer in the Forest.

These are spiritual pictures! They set the general and the mythical free from the particular, penetrating reality itself, and communicating through suitable means an experience that could not be reproduced but only be evoked. If we consider the means, we find a painting field which is moved by plastic forces, and in which atmosphere has been transformed into crystalline light, color, arabesque; sign and symbol are coordinated with sure expressive means. Every formal element functions descriptively and also supports the order of expression. Out of the indissoluble union of these elements is born a magic face of color and light that is a vehicle for all the poetic transformations.

It has embedded in it the signs of reference that lead back to the original experience in nature. What is evoked finally is the certain sense of the immanent unity of the universe. In Marc's eyes, bursting the bounds of the visible did not do injury to creation; it was just at this point that there arose the hope of experiencing the "underlying mystic design" behind natural appearances. Marc expresses this thought very clearly in a statement of 1913: "Longing for indivisible Being, liberation from the errors of sense in our ephemeral life is the basic mood of all art. Its great goal is to dissolve the entire system of our partial sensation, to show an earthly Being that dwells behind everything."

Marc's approach is very clear; he begins by choosing simple and typical forms taken from the bewildering multiplicity of nature; by means of these typical forms, given emphasis by repetition, he seeks to set up a classic rhythm which will correspond to the pulsating rhythmic quality of a living nature. In 1910, under the influence of Macke, Kandinsky, and Jawlensky, he became aware of the expressive possibilities of color. And in 1911 with the painting Red Horses he took his decisive steps, freeing color from nature and, by the act of contemplation, raising it to the higher level of a symbol. But this new independent life of color also required a new formal organization. Cubism, and in particular Delaunay's high-colored Orphism, were of assistance in this task,

Marc: Tower of Blue Horses. 1913.
Oil on canvas, 78 $^3/_4$ × 51 $^1/_4$".
Formerly in collection of National Gallery,
Berlin, present whereabouts unknown (*)

Marc: Deer in a Flower Garden. 1913. Oil on canvas, $21\,^5/_8 \times 29\,^7/_8''$. Kunsthalle, Bremen

Marc: Tyrol. 1913-14. Oil on canvas, 53 ³/₈ × 57″. Bayerische Staatsgemäldesammlungen, Munich

around 1912. Marc's great plastic images then pressed toward a unity with his pantheistic religious feeling. But once taken, this direction, which was reinforced by Kandinsky's example, led Marc to abandon objective pictures entirely. The last step toward abstract painting was made in 1914; then the experience of nature and the world entered into an even broader sphere of feeling. Marc at this time wrote in his diary: "What had previously been taken as 'pictorial material' by our passion, now is reduced to simple numerical relationships and vibrations." But war broke out, and Marc fell at Verdun in March 1916.

August Macke (1887-1914) similarly found his personal style during these years and was stimulated by the same sources. He was far more uninhibited than Marc; all his senses were directed toward the beauty of nature. For him to paint was "to go through Nature rejoicing." As early as 1907 he came upon Matisse's lyrical color in Paris and, after 1910, in contact with his friends in the Blaue Reiter, he achieved a spiritual mastery of color that enabled him to transform the visible world into poetry. In 1912 he met Delaunay, and Delaunay's Orphism taught him to articulate his emotion through a pictorial order based on subtle color relationships. Macke always had something bright, clear, and crystalline before his eyes, and his actual picture of the world was lyrically transformed on canvas by that instinctive vision. From the indications supplied by Delaunay and from his own angle of vision, Macke, in a marvelous, poetic penetration of visible nature, developed the brilliant series of pictures of 1913, subjects from the Thuner See, women looking out the window, pedestrians, children in the park (pages 62-63). Here his feelings of intense joyousness reached a highly personal expression. In the spring of 1914 he traveled with Paul Klee and Louis Molliet to Tunis. In the precious series of watercolors which followed, Macke succeeded in making each picture a plastic metaphor of the pure, ordered beauty of the world, and his subjects acquired poetic and legendary qualities. But here too death interrupted a development that was only in its beginnings; Macke died in Champagne in September 1914, but many of his thoughts lived on in Paul Klee and were matured by him.

The trip to Tunis with Macke was very important for Paul Klee (1879-1940); it released in him his gift for color. Klee's role in the Blaue Reiter is a very special one. In 1914 he had no real oeuvre to his credit, and yet his genius was already operating as the moral court of judgment among these Blaue Reiter painters who were so dedicated to high ideals. He patiently awaited the steady growth for which he seemed destined, and set down the stages of this slow evolution in small drawings, in paintings on glass, and little watercolors. When in the autumn of 1911 he joined the Blaue Reiter group, he had just drawn illustrations for Voltaire's "Candide." These tremulous figures, released by the further development of Klee's line, arose directly out of a "well-spring of psychic improvisation." The lines, feeling their way like tentacles over the luminous surface of the paper, materialized into leaping, wispy scenes. Line as an instrument of psychic

Macke: The Dress Shop. 1913. Oil on canvas, $19^7/_8 \times 23^5/_8$″. Collection Mrs. Gisela Macke, Bonn

Macke: Girls under Trees, 1914. Oil on canvas, $47\,^1/_4 \times 63''$. Kunsthaus, Zurich, on loan from private collection

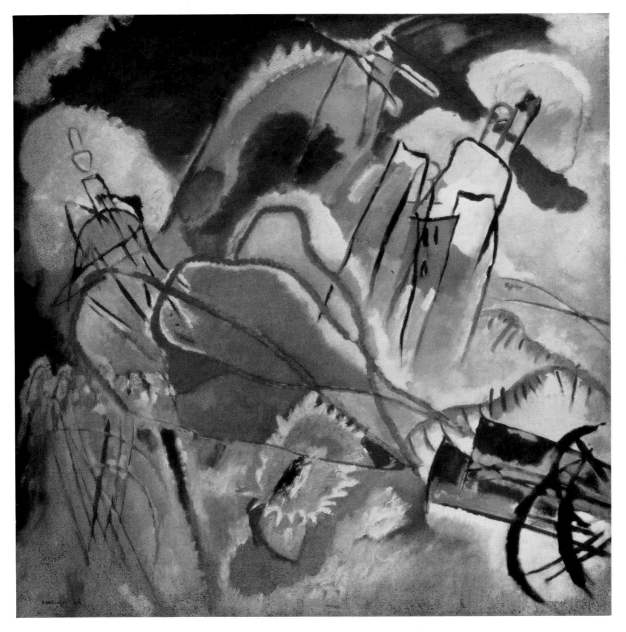

Kandinsky: Improvisation No. 30 (Warlike Theme). 1913. Oil on canvas, $43\,^1/_4 \times 43\,^3/_4''$. The Art Institute of Chicago, Arthur Jerome Eddy Memorial Collection

Kandinsky: Composition. 1913. Oil on canvas, $34\,^1/_2 \times 39\,^1/_4''$. Room of Contemporary Art, Albright Art Gallery, Buffalo, New York

1910-11 one could even find a relationship to Wagner's great operatic compositions. Just as Wagner's music is saturated with sensuous and symbolic allusions and evokes images of large scenery and figurative analogies in the listener's mind, so the waves of color in these first incunabula of abstract painting conjure up a whole inventory of material associations: symbols of walking forms, horsemen jumping, sturdy Russian churches, dramatic or bucolic scenic backgrounds. If the eye follows the epic course of the sonorous colors, it is continually confronted by these individual figurative symbols, leitmotifs, as it were, of a dramatic composition for the stage: movements of mystical color which seek to make a dramatic state of the soul visible, but do not yet sufficiently trust their independence from representation to be able to entirely abandon objective reference. Such naturalistic and sentimental residues still muddy the over-all formal organization. This fact emerges most clearly in the spatial organization which still has a naturalistic character, as of a corridor, in the perspective gradations from foreground to background. But the painting changes as early as 1911. The scheme of lines that determines the form is woven into the tempestuous colored background in a free arabesque. And now, too, the attempt to produce illusions of space disappear. The picture seems to soar away from terrestrial perspective, with its simple arrangement of foreground, middle ground, background, into a cosmic perspective in which this clear recession is replaced by and merges into a more complicated space. 1912-13 is the period in which Kandinsky vigorously came to terms with the pictorial organization of the young Frenchmen. In his paintings of 1913 (pages 68-69) we see illusionistic space give way to a shallow pictorial depth which does not observe traditional perspective, a system of stepwise layers of space and interpenetrating planes. The comparison with Cubism is obvious, but in that comparison we recognize the way in which Kandinsky gives this relatively rational system, with its calculated architecture, a very broad tension in a highly expressive way by irrationally puncturing and opening up space. Kinetic forms of motion bring a space-time element into the painting. In this way the orchestration of a new kind of picture is created, embracing both the rational and the irrational, the finite and the infinite, the static and the dynamic; the unbridled force of the North European-Eastern world of expression has erupted in an Orphic song. If one had to choose a stylistic designation for this art, it could only be called Abstract Expressionism.

The Origin of Abstract Painting

What had been achieved, then, was the discovery of a plastic procedure which made the expressive inner world of man immediately visible without having to resort metaphorically to the images of the outer world. But how was that possible? In point of fact, these ideas had long been prepared for in Germany and were, moreover, influential

Kandinsky: Composition (3). 1914. Oil on canvas,
64 × 36 1/4". The Museum of Modern Art,
New York, Mrs. Simon Guggenheim Fund

Corinth: Self Portrait. 1924. Oil on canvas, $39\,^3/_8 \times 31\,^5/_8''$. The Museum of Modern Art, gift of Curt Valentin

Corinth: Winter at Walchensee. 1924.
Watercolor, 16 × 18¹/₄″. Collection Mr. and Mrs.
Erich Cohn, New York

below, Corinth: Near the Walchensee – Silver
Way. 1923. Oil on canvas, 23¹/₄ × 35″. Collection
Mr. and Mrs. Erich Cohn, New York

Kokoschka: Portrait of Dr. Tietze and His Wife. 1909. Oil on canvas, $30\,^1/_8 \times 53\,^5/_8''$. The Museum of Modern Art, New York, Mrs. John D. Rockefeller, Jr. Fund

throughout Europe. Kandinsky came to abstract painting in 1910, but only a year later Larionoff in Moscow arrived at abstraction, and in 1912 Delaunay and Kupka did so in Paris, all quite independently of Kandinsky. Nonetheless, it was Kandinsky who came upon the earliest and most valid results in Munich!

I have already pointed out that the problem of abstract form had been raised quite openly in the esthetic of the Munich Jugendstil; as early as the beginning of the century, Obrist and Endell had concerned themselves with non-objective ornamental sculpture, and Hölzel in 1906 experimented with abstract ornament in painting. In the same year Kubin, frightened and fascinated by a glance into a microscope, painted a series of abstract pictures resembling bundles of filmy material and crystals or shell-like fragments. And in his novel "Die Andere Seite" (1908-09) Kubin has a painter (in some ways autobiographic) ponder over a "fragmentary, calligraphic style that would express the slightest tremors of mood, like a sensitive meteorological instrument." The correspondence between Marc and Macke in 1910 is constantly concerned with the abstract powers of color and the psychological effects of their pure tones. There is also the case of Ciurlionis, the Lithuanian, who as early as 1905 seriously took up the comparison of color and musical tones, a common topic in the painters' studios of that time, and painted compositions that grew increasingly abstract in a kind of symphonic movement, Sea Sonata, Sun Sonata, etc. Out of his abstract-cosmic vision he created forms which resembled heavenly bodies moving in infinite spaces, shot through with Jugendstil arabesques and rhythms. This whole development is not altogether surprising if we think of Odilon Redon, the "peintre symphonique," or Klimt. It is merely a reflection, carried to a characteristic extreme, of a particularly enthusiastic, ornamental aspect of the Jugendstil. The core of new truth that lay behind such merely groping or romantic experiments was worked out with the clearest consciousness by Kandinsky, whose gifts of intuition and intelligence developed it into a solid spiritual patrimony.

Personal elements also entered into the matter. Kandinsky was a Russian, and the symbolic language of the icon, the mystical splendor of the Orthodox Church, the variegated ornament of Russian folk art were deeply rooted in his sensibility. From time immemorial the mystical element in Russian humanity had expressed itself in sensuous images set against the abstract background of the surface. Moreover, Kandinsky had an extraordinary sensitivity to the living essence of pure color, and this was connected with his great powers of synesthism. As a young student in Moscow he had heard Wagner's "Lohengrin," and he was able to translate musical sound into a play of colors, writing, "I realized that painting has the same power as music." He then reacted to developments in modern painting itself. When, during his youth in Moscow, he saw a painting of a haystack by Monet, he did not at first recognize the object depicted at all, but was conscious of experiencing a vivid pictorial presence, a picture, whose purely

Kokoschka: Dent du Midi. 1910. Oil on canvas, 31 $^1/_8$ × 45 $^1/_4$″. Collection Mrs. W. Feilchenfeldt, Zurich

painterly means were of such intensity as to leave the object represented quite uninteresting. His plastic thinking evolved through a chain of development extending from Impressionism through Gauguin and the Neo-Impressionists to the Fauves. All of Kandinsky's work from 1905 to 1910 was devoted to finding a solution step-by-step to Gauguin's question, "Why should we not be able to create color harmonies that correspond to the state of our souls?" And the answer finally culminated in pure abstract painting.

Now, strangely enough, the solution seemed especially to coincide with the great changes of ideas in modern science. With the splitting of the atom, old concepts of matter were replaced by concepts of energy, and the traditional solidity of objects gave

Kokoschka: Portrait of Herwarth Walden. 1910. Oil on canvas, $39\,^1/_2 \times 27\,^1/_4''$. Collection Mr. and Mrs. Samuel H. Maslon, Wayzata, Minnesota (through the courtesy of the Minneapolis Institute of Arts)

way to the idea of the field of force. Furthermore there was the necessity, as it proved, of introducing the concept of space-time; it transformed the static perspective system, by which observed reality had been understood visually since the Renaissance, into a dynamic picture of the world which discarded traditional perspective. These new scientific premises gave unexpected confirmation to the suspicions of the painter that visual reality consisted only in the human capacity for perception and found its counterpart in an inner representation. When Kandinsky heard in his youth of the achievement of smashing the atom, he wrote, "The discovery hit me with frightful force, as though the end of the world had come. All things became transparent, without strength or certainty." At that moment the chain binding the painter to visible things broke, for now the abandonment of natural appearances no longer meant that the artist despised or violated creation; on the contrary, it had become necessary to bring the new and broader conception of the universe into artistic vision.

This belief in the possibility of rendering in pictorial terms the "underlying mystical design of the visible world" gives the Blaue Reiter painters their great significance. Out of their approach came the abstract and hermetic painting which formed the new attitudes of modern man to plastic reality, and to these attitudes Kandinsky and Klee gave a world-wide authority.

Oskar Kokoschka

But further desire for knowledge was in the modern spirit. It was directed immediately toward man and his inner being. Through Munch and Strindberg it had already been made clear, artistically, that man does not exist on a narrow plane that is free of doubts. This intuitive probing of the inner world of man through art was now powerfully confirmed by the science of psychoanalysis founded by Freud in Vienna. And out of the milieu of the Vienna Jugendstil came the painter, Oskar Kokoschka (born 1886), who had an incomparable capacity for uncovering images beneath the sensitive skin of natural appearances. At the point of strongest psychological tension Kokoschka bored in, as it were, and came up with – the self portrait.

His early pictures, of the period 1908-09, are immediately recognizable representations of still lifes and portraits. But the visual reality of objects and faces within these works really represents the psychological state of the painter, and this is achieved by a hallucinatory manipulation of the painter's objects. His portraits are sketches of human faces made half in a trance, and they disclose more about the painter and his humanity than they do about the model. For this reason all the models resemble each other in their spiritual condition. The eye of the painter looking at a man suddenly conceives something phantasmal in him, a play of gesture, some piece of mimicry caught on the wing,

Kokoschka: The Power of Music (Die Macht der Musik). 1919. Oil on canvas, $40\,^1/_8 \times 59''$. Stedelijk van Abbe-museum, Eindhoven, Holland

which takes the place of the subject, and which the artist relentlessly isolates and penetrates. This response of the painter stands in direct relationship to himself alone. His painting is, to be sure, a visual impression, but there is behind this, submerged, an element of second-sight, another aspect of the artist's reality – it is a revelation of himself. Kokoschka attempts to illustrate this vision with the means at the disposal of painting. This is objectively expressed in the portraits by means of grimace and gesture, and hence the emphasis on the head as the scene of mimicry and of the hand as the scene of gesture (page 74). The means themselves are an Impressionism made ecstatic; the graphic elements become nervous and hectic, and the color feverish and phantasmagoric.

The goal of the picture is the most expressive possible illustration of a vision that has been torn out of the feelings, and an impression even though, as may happen, the organic body of the picture itself is in shreds. The painters of the Brücke, those of the Blaue Reiter, and Nolde all sought to transform a visual experience into painting. Kokoschka came from the other side of reality, from a world that objectified dream and vision. It was his genius to show the visionary possibilities of German Expressionism.

The Answer of the Environment

All these new anti-naturalistic movements in the new German painting won many followers in an astonishingly short time. A group of German painters gathered around Matisse in Paris as early as 1908, Purrmann, Levi, Moll, and in the Rhineland another center of a more French-oriented expressionism (Chagall, Matisse) took form with Thorn-Prikker, Helmuth Macke, Campendonk, Nauen, and Morgner, who was killed in action at an early age. The older masters of German Impressionism, and especially Lovis Corinth, also let themselves be drawn along a little way, and the broad public soon became aware of the new directions in painting. In the summer of 1912 the great Sonderbund show in Cologne brought together the entire constellation of European modernism for the first time. Van Gogh, Cézanne, and Munch had rooms to themselves. Around them were grouped the new European painting: Picasso, the French, Swiss, English, and Dutch. Against this world background there now appeared the Expressionists of the Berlin New Secession, the painters of the Blaue Reiter and the Brücke. This ensemble was an impressive documentation of the range of the new styles in Europe.

Berlin had become a powerful propaganda center, marshaling the new forces. There in 1910 Herwarth Walden founded the magazine Der Sturm. Originally it had been conceived rather as a militant literary organ, but it soon became a recruiting medium for the new European painting. Walden had brought Kokoschka to Berlin in 1910 and published in Der Sturm a large number of his masterly Expressionist portrait drawings in a series called "Portrait of the Week." In 1911 the artists of the Brücke contributed to Der Sturm as did also in 1912, those of the Blaue Reiter. By 1913 Paul Klee's first drawings appeared on the title pages of the magazine. And then, in 1912, Walden attached a gallery of his own to the editorial offices, and in rapid succession showed a solid chain of the new artists: Kokoschka, the Blaue Reiter, the Futurists, the German Expressionists, the French Cubists, and Orphists, Ensor, Delaunay, Archipenko. In the autumn of 1913, the same year in which the famous Armory Show was held in New York, introducing the modern movement to the United States, Herwarth Walden summed up his gallery activity in the first German Autumn Salon. The show contained 360 works, with the paintings of Henri Rousseau in the place of honor. In fraternal proximity to the works

Kokoschka: London Bridge: View of the Thames. 1925-26. Oil on canvas, $35^{3}/_{8} \times 51^{1}/_{4}$". Room of Contemporary Art, Albright Art Gallery, Buffalo

of the German innovators were hung those of the Italian Futurists, the French Cubists, Chagall, Delaunay, Brancusi, Archipenko, and Epstein; Mondrian was also represented and so were Max Ernst and Hans Arp. With an amazing sureness of touch, Walden had brought together almost all the forces that had determined or were to determine the over-all picture of modern art. And this demonstration of the great unified stylistic tendency, covering all countries, was of the greatest significance. It can be said that after the Sonderbund exhibition and the Autumn Salon the significance of modern painting in Germany could no longer be overlooked.

The War and the New Realism

Then came the war, interrupting this fortunate and continuous development. It left many great gaps. Marc, Macke and Morgner fell; Kandinsky and Jawlensky left Germany. Almost all the painters were at the front for years. Hofer was in a prison camp in France; Kirchner had a nervous breakdown and was taken to Switzerland, critically ill. The experience of the war changed humanity. When Germany collapsed, it was not only a war that was lost; the entire political, social, and philosophical structure broke down. The disintegrations in the social sphere, however, had less significance for the new formal structure of art. Changes of systems of expression occur outside of political life; moreover, the artists had long since assimilated the war in their revolutionary transformation. In 1916 Paul Klee set down the following thought: "I have had this war within me for a long time, and therefore it does not affect me inwardly at all." Thus the claim of the new expressive painting and its continuity of thought were conserved; but the spiritual condition of humanity and temporal events, disturbing to artistic man, had changed.

The influences that did arise from the war operated in two directions. Immediately afterwards there was felt in all the countries of Europe a need for serenity, for the stately calm of the classic, for a quieter dialogue with nature. I have already pointed out that at the beginning of the third decade, the foremost Expressionists, Nolde, Rohlfs, Heckel, Schmidt-Rottluff, and even Kirchner, also began to draw back to a less agitated mode of conceiving nature and a more serene and monumental pictorial architecture. Kokoschka too, after the first hectic outbreaks of his temperament, found his way to a dramatic Impressionism that corresponded to his more relaxed and joyful mood of adoration before nature.

At the same time one had to digest the terrifying experience of trench warfare, a brutally immediate reality, and also to absorb the Utopian dogmas of mass welfare which rose like bubbles from this quagmire, and which were in contrast to the overwhelming harshness of the German post-war world. Man's outlook became stern and bitter, preoccupied with the dark side of social life. Profiteers, pimps, prostitutes, the mutilated, the wretched flotsam of the war were compelling subjects for pictures with which one could actively moralize. Art become a weapon of attack and defense.

This socially critical realism which at the outset had connections with the expressive means of Futurism, Dadaism, and the Italian "pittura metafisica" was introduced by George Grosz (born 1893). More a draftsman than a painter, he had built up out of suggestions from Pascin, Kokoschka, and Klee, an apparently childlike, but actually sophisticated, linear style, with which he tersely depicted reality. From Futurism and

opposite, Grosz: Funeral of the Poet Panizza. 1917-18. Oil on canvas, $55^1/_8 \times 43^1/_4$". Staatliche Kunstsammlungen, Stuttgart

82

Grosz: Café Neptun. c. 1920. Watercolor, 18 1/2 × 14 1/2″. The Art
Institute of Chicago, Olivia Shaler Swan Fund

Grosz: In Rue Blondel. 1925. Watercolor, 18 1/4 × 16″. Collection
Mr. and Mrs. Erich Cohn, New York

Dadaism Grosz adopted the technique of simultaneous vision, in order to interweave
individual satirical images in the whole rhythm of metropolitan life (page 83). He now
set the striking power of these means to work in the service of his biting topical satire,
aggressively representing the basest aspects of the reality of his times. In the process
the elements of caricature and satirical realism more and more displaced a Futurist
and Dada stylistic vocabulary. From this emerged the candid, reportorial style of a critically observing realist, whose sardonic images expressed his discontent with the age.

Another bitter realist arose in this violent German Expressionist climate, Otto Dix
(born 1891). His glance, which had become hardened and accusing in the face of the
horrors of trench warfare experienced as a front line soldier, now discovered the same
terror everywhere in naked reality. This reality was not to be evoked by "art." Only
the dissonant and the very gross could bring to a heightened clarity such a tortured

84

Grosz: The Poet Max Hermann-Neisse. 1927. Oil on canvas, $23\,^3/_8 \times 29\,^1/_8''$. The Museum of Modern Art, New York

Now Max Ernst (born 1891) took up this theme of the new relationships of things. He left "art" out entirely. He drew on material that already existed, that was prefabricated, and "ready-made." He was fascinated by the magical, sharp reality of the technical drawings in the catalogues put out by the machine industry, and the engravings of scientific textbooks. The intense reality of these illustrations cast a spell and tempted him to manipulate the prefabricated pictures in order to make their harsh reality more eloquent by means of irrational juxtapositions (below). If one cut these pictures out and rearranged them freshly, as a fascinated curiosity might dictate, the elements of the fantastic automatically emerged. Montages of a precise verisimilitude were formed, which became dream pictures by the confusion of representation of objects, objects which were transformed into magical presences. These prefabricated pictures were used to form an astonishing world of marvels in an absurd realistic style; a poetic reinterpre-

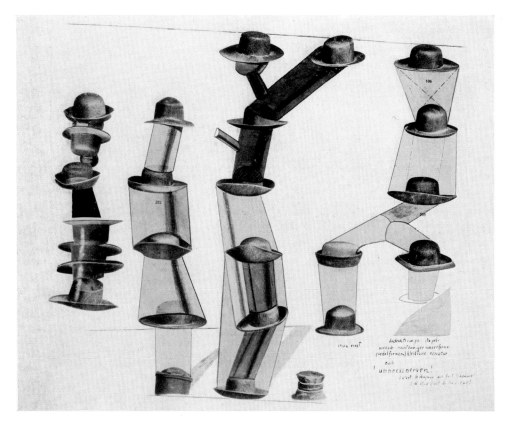

Ernst: The Hat Makes the Man. 1920. Collage, pencil, ink, watercolor, 14 × 18". The Museum of Modern Art, New York

Ernst: The Gramineous Bicycle Garnished with Bells the Dappled Fire Damps and the Echinoderms Bending the Spine to Look for Caresses. 1920 or '21. Anatomical chart altered with gouache, $29^1/_4 \times 39^1/_4''$. The Museum of Modern Art

tation was achieved by the arbitrary coincidence of elements of reality. In these montages one basic aim of veristic Surrealism was already achieved. When Ernst moved to Paris in 1922, this idea of an irrational manipulation of facsimiles of objects, in order to provoke the strongest poetic effects, had penetrated deeply into international Surrealism.

Out of a similar feeling for the mystery of commonplace things, Kurt Schwitters (1887-1948) in Hanover discovered a new variation on Dada paintings in about 1920. He no longer set form against form, but material against material. With marvelous witchery, he collected every kind of waste and scrap and imaginatively put them together to form compositions (pages 93-95). Out of these remnants he made new objects in which the juxtapositon of diverse details, created a new atmosphere of reality.

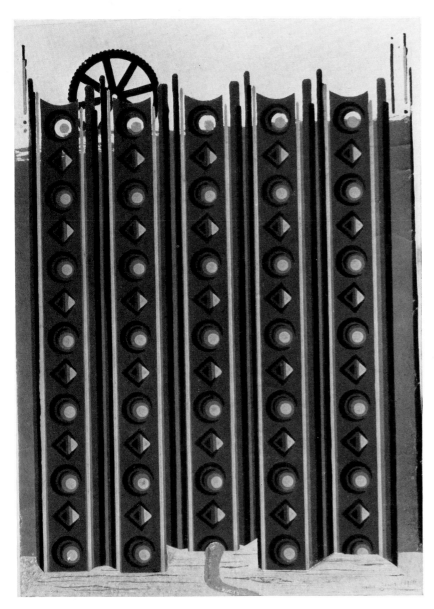

Ernst: The Little Tear Gland That Says Tic Tac. 1920. Gouache on wallpaper,
14¼ × 10″. The Museum of Modern Art, New York

Schwitters: Drawing R 2: Hansi-Schokolade. 1918. Collage of colored papers and wrapper, $7^1/_8 \times 5^3/_4''$. The Museum of Modern Art, New York

Schwitters: Merz 448: Moscow. 1922. Collage of cardboard and wood, $6 \times 6^1/_4''$. The Museum of Modern Art, New York, Katherine S. Dreier Bequest

Schwitters: Merz Construction. 1921. Collage, painted wood, wire, paper, $14^1/_2 \times 8^1/_2$". Philadelphia Museum of Art, A. E. Gallatin Collection, Pennsylvania

Schwitters: Merz 2005: Constantinople. 1924. Collage of cut paper, cardboard, tram tickets, pellet of wood, $5^1/_8 \times 4^1/_8$". The Museum of Modern Art, New York, Katherine S. Dreier Bequest

Schwitters: Picture with Light Center. 1919. Paper collage with oil on cardboard, $33\,^1/_4 \times 25\,^7/_8''$.
The Museum of Modern Art, New York

This novel relationship of objects and an expressive realism, romantically diluted, gave rise to the Neue Sachlichkeit which Hartlaub in 1925 brought together in a great exhibition in his gallery in Mannheim. It corresponded to the classic-realistic tendencies among the Italians ("valori plastici") and the French (Derain, Picasso) and was broadly conceived, but it did not bring to light any name worthy of particular mention.

This trend, however, contributed to the development of the pictorial world of Carl Hofer (1878-1955), whose painting was characterized by a spare and disillusioned idealism. The starting point for Hofer was Hans von Marées and Cézanne, and he believed that in his long residences in India (in 1909 and 1911) he had found a lyrical ideal of figure painting. But friction with the realities of life, the war, his internment for years as a prisoner, the bitter atmosphere of the post-war period, crushed the shell of his idyll. The ideal of maidenhood was replaced by the suburban girl, and the place of a glowing fleshiness was often taken by a mask. His paintings became sober, without sensuousness and their bare structure was open to the light of day. A dry color with few accents built up the flat background. A few themes always recur and in the course of this repetition, the organization of the pictures becomes more ascetic. This quality in German art between the two wars is a special accent. Hofer was a painter who began with a dream of ideal beauty which contact with reality shattered. Out of this disenchantment came his pictures which were also interpretations of his times.

Max Beckmann

The most powerful figure in this trend of the time toward a new definition of reality was Max Beckmann (1884-1950). The war confronted him too with its stern truths, and forced him to give up the early style that he had developed in the Impressionist climate of the Berlin Secession. An inexorable determination to state facts kept him squarely facing reality. Once more it was the tangible object or figure that led to a new artistic statement. Physical reality was that which could be grasped and precisely determined as a volume. If the visible were disrobed, and pure and simple form defined, these shapes then attained an unusually powerful emblematic presence, becoming suitable material for the construction of reality. However, since forms were defined as sculptured volumes, they entered into an intrinsic contradiction with their surrounding space. It was precisely the solidity of Beckmann's reality that gave space, by contrast, its empty, limitless, uncertain character, and made it the locus of the gods and of anxiety. In order to break down this void, Beckmann struggled to find a new arithmetic of solid things; what had to be done, he said, was to put a jumble of things in front of the emptiness of space, so that its fearful depth would not be seen. The drama of every picture by Beckmann arises out of the tension between the objects and space.

Hofer: Three Clowns. 1922. Oil on canvas, 51 $\frac{1}{4}$ × 41 $\frac{3}{8}$″. Wallraf-Richartz Museum, Cologne

Hofer: Houses at Montagnola. 1926. Oil on canvas, $25\,^3/_4 \times 31\,^7/_8''$. Niedersächsische Landesgalerie, Hanover

opposite, Hofer : Early Hour. 1935. Oil on canvas, $49\,^1/_4 \times 61\,^3/_8''$. Portland Art Museum, Oregon

In these pictures, objects and figures are seen in emphatic contour and strong volume, each an isolated presence asserting its own powers of existence. Every volume pushes into space individually and supports itself against the next. The separate volumes build up with brute force the spatial scheme which becomes its own convincing reality. Emptiness is filled with interlocking forms which check the movement of space. And the collision between space and volumes form the drama of the picture. We do not have an imitative reproduction of reality represented by means of real facts, but a structured reality built up of real facts. On this pictorial stage which criss-crossed and framed the painting surface, Beckmann then began to let objects and figures come together in allegory, fables of human life that are quite plausible and convincingly made. If it often happened that the allegory could not be resolved at every point, it always had the immediate value of a metaphor of an existential experience of reality.

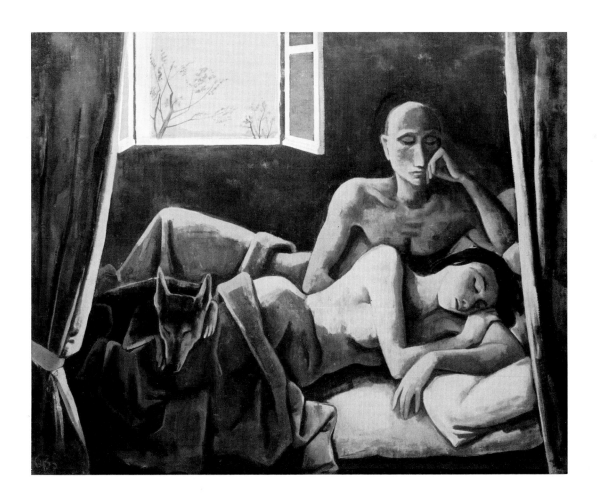

Beckmann encountered Expressionism about 1917 but at once attempted to combine it with an aggressive realism, somewhat in Grosz' direction. Cubism, and the late German Gothic masters' system of spatial division, helped him to work out his dramatic, lattice-like space. Henri Rousseau taught him the magical nobility of simply defined objects. From 1920 Beckmann built up his motif with emblematic pictorial symbols. Piece by piece, in a hard, naive determination to define, he found for himself the form and volume of the object, fitting it into the construction of the picture. Forms are established by drawing; color seems to have been merely added. He often made trips to Paris, and after 1928 he allowed a blooming coloration to grow slowly in his paintings. This was the final step from a graphic treatment of form to a more painterly definition. In this new phase the stern preoccupations with contour, volume, space, and color came to a forceful conclusion. Beckmann now expressed intuitively the entire content of his experience of reality in magnificent paintings. Great triptychs became the stage for his figure groups and for the dark allegoric scenes in which Beckmann locked his experience of existence (pages 104-105).

Beckmann: View of Genoa. 1927. Oil on canvas, 35 $^1/_2$ × 66 $^1/_2$″. Collection Mr. and Mrs. Morton D. May, St. Louis, Missouri

opposite, Beckmann: Family Picture. 1920. Oil on canvas, 25 $^5/_8$ × 39 $^3/_4$″.
The Museum of Modern Art, New York, gift of Mrs. John D. Rockefeller Jr.

opposite, Beckmann: The Bath. 1931. Oil on canvas, 70 × 48″. Collection Mr. and Mrs. Morton D. May, St. Louis, Missouri

Beckmann: Rugby Players. 1929. Oil on canvas, 84 7/8 × 39 3/8″. Städtisches Museum, Duisburg

Beckmann: Temptation. 1936. Oil on canvas; triptych,
center panel 79 × 67″, side panels each 84³/₄ × 39¹/₄″.
Collection Dr. Stephan Lackner, Santa Barbara, California

Beckmann's greatness lies in the inexorable way in which he gave expression to his own vision of reality and to his position in the world. But this evocation of an external reality was at the same time a self-invocation. "The real love for the things outside of us and the deep secrets of events within us," as he put it, came to characteristic synthesis. Beckmann called this method of his "transcendental realism."

The Painters of the Bauhaus

The new efforts to arrive at a plastic definition of contemporary experience can be understood as a further development of the Expressionist view of nature. Now the ideas concerning Orphic and abstract paintings that had sprung up in the Blaue Reiter were developed further and brought to striking maturity. They found their concentrated center of action in the Bauhaus.

At the beginning of 1919 in Weimar, Walter Gropius, an architect, had founded the Bauhaus, an institution that in research and instruction took for its theme the forming of the entire human environment through architecture, industrial design, painting, and sculpture. The fine and applied arts were seen to grow out of present-day practical circumstances, determined by technology as well as by spiritual conditions. The fine arts studios were thought of as a kind of emancipated creative center, the chambers of the heart, from which the elevated and free artistic impulses were to penetrate into the utilitarian world of the workshops. With marvelous sureness of touch, Gropius brought together the most sensitive painters, those who were thinking through the problem of form most keenly. In 1919 Lyonel Feininger was invited to the Bauhaus; in 1921, Paul Klee and Oskar Schlemmer; in 1922 Kandinsky followed, and in 1923, Moholy-Nagy.

Kandinsky and Klee came directly from the Blaue Reiter; Feininger and Schlemmer were also close to the circle. Moholy-Nagy and Kandinsky (who had just returned from Russia) brought to this artistic forum the ideas of Russian Constructivism and the Dutch de Stijl movement. Van Doesburg, Mondrian, Malevich, El Lissitzky, Naum Gabo had close personal relationships with the Bauhaus. The Orphism of the Blaue Reiter and Constructivism balanced each other fruitfully. Basically this remained the key, although a Constructivist purism, and the emphasis on industrial design which developed out of it, slowly came to the fore and produced serious tensions.

In 1925 the Bauhaus moved to Dessau. Gropius left in 1928, and the Bauhaus went through a grave internal crisis. Schlemmer accepted a call to Breslau in 1929; in 1930 Klee went to Düsseldorf. Mies van der Rohe in 1930 tried to recapture the old Bauhaus spirit. But meanwhile the Bauhaus had become the target of the cultural program of rising national socialism. Then in 1932 the institution retreated to Berlin and was closed there in May of 1933 as a "hotbed of cultural Bolshevism."

Feininger: The Side Wheeler. 1913. Oil on canvas, $34^3/_4 \times 39^5/_8''$. The Detroit Institute of Arts, Michigan

The emigration of the men of the Bauhaus now began. Gropius, Mies van der Rohe, Moholy-Nagy, Herbert Bayer, Marcel Breuer departed for the United States. Kandinsky moved to Paris, and Klee to Bern. Although today the name of the Bauhaus has almost become synonymous with functionalism in architecture, Constructivism in the plastic arts, and industrial design, its identification solely with these developments is a quite erroneous limitation of its spiritual range. The works and the teachings of its four great painters – Kandinsky, Klee, Schlemmer, Feininger – made a unique and genuine contribution to modern painting, which was to inscribe the name of the Bauhaus firmly in the annals of the history of the fine arts as well. What took place there on the highest artistic plane was the extension of the ideas that Kandinsky and Klee had begun to set forth in the Blaue Reiter. Feininger and Schlemmer also shared in this accomplishment.

Lyonel Feininger (1871-1956) exhibited with the Blaue Reiter in the Berlin Autumn Salon of 1913. In Cubism Feininger found the harmony, discipline, and order that corresponded to his personality, but at the same time his romantic feeling for nature required him to make this strict order poetic. In 1911 he became acquainted with Delaunay and now recognized in Orphic Cubism the lyrical possibilities of the Cubist formula. And through Delaunay's architectural pictures, he found his way to his preferred themes. The evolution from Orphism to the Blaue Reiter, with its idea of an "underlying mystical design," was only logical.

In his Bauhaus paintings, Feininger worked to clarify his Cubism, which was initially very dynamic. Fine-layered and transparent planes create a cool spatial crystal, in which the play of clear horizontals and verticals are held in asymmetrical balance. Constructive directional lines and fine points of support, where Feininger likes to put a human figure as a punctuation, define this clear spatial geometry. The pictorial design, composed like a fugue, recaptures the crystalline vision of the Gothic architecture of the old German cities (page 111). The transparent structure of the picture transforms the motif into visual poetry. In Feininger's seascapes a great open space and a mirrored atmosphere are fixed in this calculated order. The lucid, magical geometry of his pictures, which sets forth infinite space in diamond-like facets, allows the romantic spirit and gentle mysticism of the Blaue Reiter to shine through clearly. In his last pictures as well (Feininger returned to his native America in 1937), the fugitive play of the atmosphere is refracted in an enchanted space.

Oskar Schlemmer (1888-1943) had no immediate contact with the Blaue Reiter, but his work too was characterized by the effort to humanize the formal, geometric painting of Cubism. He wanted to preserve an image of man at the center of the geometrical orders, as a humanist symbol joining the rational and the mystical. And so with purist rigor he composed his paintings, setting a formalized idol in the midst of a world of three-dimensional geometry, an idol of man as a symbol of a supra-individual.

Feininger: Bridge III. 1917. Oil on canvas, $31\,^1/_2 \times 39\,^3/_8''$. Wallraf-Richartz Museum, Cologne

Feininger: The Steamer "Odin," II. 1927. Oil on canvas. $26^1/_2 \times 39^1/_2$". The Museum of Modern Art, New York, acquired through the Lillie P. Bliss Bequest

Feininger: Barfüsser Church in Erfurt. 1927. Oil on canvas, $39 \times 31^1/_4$". Collection Dr. Ferdinand Ziersch, Wuppertal-Barmen

Schlemmer: Five Men in a Room. 1928.
Oil on canvas, $59 \times 35\,^3/_8''$.
Collection Dr. Max Fischer, Stuttgart

When Schlemmer came to the Bauhaus, he undertook a class in stage design. He was passionately devoted to the theater and the dance, and in those years was working on the completion of his Constructivist "Triadic Ballet." He was now able to have his mannequin-like figures appear actively in the imaginary, artificial space of the theater. Schlemmer had learned that the figures which he executed as a dancer introduced a human element of tension into the formalistic space of the theater. It was these spatial configurations that Schlemmer, as painter, wished to put into permanent form (page 114). And thus there occur in his pictures groups of figures set on various planes; the inter-

Schlemmer: Group in Cut-Out View (Gruppe im Ausschnitt). 1930. Oil on canvas, 44 × 35″. Rose Fried Gallery, New York

Schlemmer: Seated Figure. 1936. Oil on canvas, $25^1/_4 \times 18^7/_8''$. Folkwang Museum, Essen

opposite, Schlemmer: Bauhaus Stairway. 1932. Oil on canvas, $63^3/_4 \times 44^3/_4''$.
The Museum of Modern Art, New York, gift of Philip C. Johnson

sections and dislocations of the planes create a spatial geometry whose irrational character reflects the inner tensions of man. His theme was "the many-sided representation of man in the abstract spaces of the future, of transparency, of mirroring." In this connection he created an icon-like figure in which the mystical relationship of man and space could be contemplated as a "symbol of a unity of nature and spirit."

A mystical conception of the unity of all being was at the core of the Blaue Reiter. Kandinsky's art drew its life from it, but when he came to the Bauhaus in 1922 not only his style, but also the purpose of his art, was greatly changed. In 1915 he had gone back to Russia and at close range lived through the experiments of the Russian Constructivists who conceived of abstract geometrical form as a concrete reality. This led him to suppress the expressive and psychologically evocative factors in his art and to assert the picture in its concrete actuality as a self-existent harmony. Carried along by the magnificent spiritual tension of the Bauhaus, which uniquely held in equilibrium the most rigorous architecture and the purest poetry, Kandinsky enthusiastically adopted this new idea. His pictures become sharply defined, bright, and of a geometrical precision (opposite). A sensitive play of balanced geometrical forms is set forth on the white surface in brilliant, unadulterated colors: circles, triangles, squares, rods, arcs, twists of line. As far as possible every form is standardized and exactly determined with T-square, triangle, and compass. The closeness to Constructivism is obvious, but still more obvious is the difference in range. The pictures now seem like musical compositions with a firm beat in rich rhythm, and they can be experienced as pure, concrete formal organizations without seeking references to objective, sensory experience. By means of such elementary forms, an autonomous, verifiable, pictorial reality is constructed with a fine regularity. Expressionism has thereby been put aside, since the artist's passions or the settling of accounts with visible nature were no longer in question. As in a musical composition, the artist has invoked and created a higher state of being, from which a gleam of a universal harmony falls into the darkness that surrounds man. Kandinsky's paintings became an instrument of the universal and a fraternal neighbor to the puritanical genius of Mondrian.

In his late Paris period (he emigrated to the French capital in 1933), Kandinsky once more showed a magnificent synthesis in a style of extraordinary scope. Then the freest intuitions united with the clearest spiritual control to achieve concrete forms that once again took on a more human content.

If we consider Kandinsky's work as a whole, it comprises the entire domain of abstract painting, ranging from abstract Expressionism to rigorous Constructivism. This was the powerful message that Kandinsky passed on to the next generation to be mastered and further developed. It is predominant today in the most significant areas of contemporary painting in the world.

Kandinsky: Composition 8, No. 260. 1923. Oil on canvas, $55^1/_2 \times 79^1/_8''$. The Solomon R. Guggenheim Museum, New York

Kandinsky: No. 678. 1940. Oil on canvas,
$39^{1}/_{4} \times 25^{1}/_{2}''$. The Solomon R. Guggenheim
Museum, New York

But there was still another artistic contribution of the Bauhaus which was to find world-wide response. It came from Paul Klee and was also based on the romantic vision of the great connections in the realm of being between the ego and the world, the earthly and the cosmic. For Klee a picture was in the highest sense a "comparison to the totality of the All." For this vision he sought a lasting intuitive symbol, an image which could serve as a formal analogy for the all-embracing unity of man and the world. To find this unifying image, which was not merely a reproduction of visible nature, he carefully prepared his expressive means, his thought, and his technique. He transformed every pictorial device – line, form, rhythm, forms of movement, space, tone, color – by the most precise analysis, freeing them from their representational function for a more evocative freedom. As the field in which these plastic forces were to appear, he produced the plane, the abstract picture surface entirely independent of nature, on which what had been evoked could be written down. He composed and moved the picture surface by his ordering of the superimposed planes, thereby creating an autonomous pictorial space which does not observe traditional rules of perspective. With the addition of color a magically illuminated, independent space of colored light appears. He now moves over this evocative surface, drawing on it with an attenuated line which in the course of its improvisation becomes a vehicle of every psychic stimulus. Heeding his own powers of association, he brings something poetic to his immediate intuitions. The results may be a nature poem about a plant, animal, or landscape, but they can also lead to an aerial or subterranean region alien to man. Or Klee may uncover merely a vague resonance, or an acrobatic, dancing movement caused by the rhythmic play of the colors themselves. Something mythical might be suggested in the tone of the colors, or Klee might let a discursive line, feeling its way among the magic zones of colors, find essences that are at home between the stars and the earth. Thus he prepared the picture surface as a vibrant sounding board and a sensitive organ which responded to poetic impulses and intuitive experience.

But these impulses and experiences arise out of a very deep realization of physical nature. A preoccupation with nature was a "conditio sine qua non" for Klee. He endeavored to orient himself precisely in the natural world. By the most exact analytic observation of nature's forms and by a penetrating contemplation of them, he developed a repertory of quintessential images. From the stock of ideas cultivated in his subconscious, there emerged on the picture surface symbols of reality of an astonishing precision; they not only reproduced the static factors in natural scenes but also the forces and genetic processes of nature: growing, blooming, streaming, swaying. It is nature deeply understood, deeply immersed in a wealth of remembered ideas that was used in the painter's vision. And so it was possible for these intimations of a complex, unified reality to reach expression through well-handled means, both reflecting the painter's

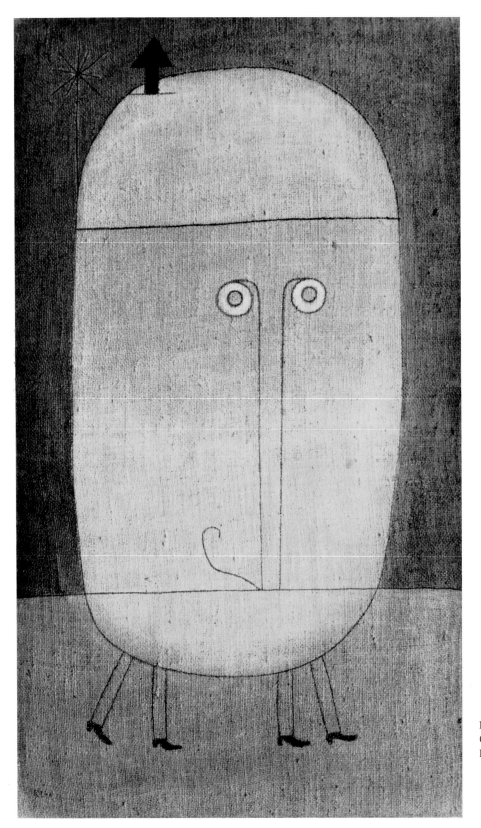

Klee: Mask of Fear (Maske Furcht). 1932.
Oil on burlap, $39\,^1/_2 \times 22\,^1/_2''$. Collection
Dr. and Mrs. Allan Roos, New York

own introspection and becoming formal symbols of something actually seen. Klee's pictures were, therefore, a self-sufficient architecture as well as a plastic image: finely tuned harmonic structures as well as illustrations of a poetic intuition of the world. They were abstract and objective at the same time.

Klee's art showed how this apparent incompatibility between the decorative and the illustrative, between architecture and image, between the abstract and the objective could be resolved. A broad new conception of the singleness and poetic wholeness of reality was revealed into which the individual components of experience entered on an equal footing: the Ego of man, the Thou of things, the Below of the terrestrial, the Above of the cosmic. Klee's small, modest papers and paintings disclosed a new vision of things which gave painting a remarkable poetic breadth and depth. That explains the fascination Klee has exercised in the last decade, and indicates why he is one of the greatest masters of the century.

The German Contribution

We see that the German contribution to European painting has been very diversified. By their powers of conviction Kandinsky and Klee brought the various lines of development in abstract painting to a flowering which fertilized all of European painting. But there were also Beckmann's "transcendental realism," Kokoschka's dramatic Impressionism, Kirchner's hieroglyphics, Klee's cultivation of a plastic alphabet that seemed to make possible the erection of a bridge between the poles of a "great reality" and a "great abstraction." With these artists German painting stood at the complex beginnings of a style.

Compared with that of the other countries of Europe, German painting showed a decidedly romantic character. The Orphic and nature mysticism, man's place in the cosmos, run through all its pictorial statements as a private theme. France's rational genius gave the new European program of modernism formal strength and clarity of style, but German painting added depth and an ideal dimension.

Totalitarianism and the Second World War

But just as this magnificent development was spreading wide and deep into the life of society, and public and private collections were opening their doors to it, it succumbed to a new political and spiritual catastrophe. In a tendency to self-destruction that obviously lies deep in the German nature, the German people destroyed the bases of their own creative freedom. Hitler and his cohorts assumed power in 1933. Persecution of the free creative spirit began.

Winter:
(Durchb
Oil on c
Owned

125

Baumeister: M

equilibrium
myths, by ga
with ancien
of content o

If we wi
mention ma
the interse
works in w
world. Repr
(born 1901)
1913), whos
we would fi
in the Hoch

Winter: Dead Forest (Toter Wald). 1953. Oil on burlap, $53\,^3/_4 \times 57\,^7/_8''$. Collection Mrs. Gertrud A. Mellon, New York

demberge-Gildenwart. Between these two positions there is a meditative school of painting reflecting the poetic power of abstract forms, of which Gerhard Fietz (born 1910) and Konrad Westphal (born 1891) might be considered representative. In contrast to this direction is a form of painting which makes full use of the dramatic, or figurative, values of abstract form, developed by Georg Meistermann (born 1911) and Josef Fassbender (born 1902). Among the younger generation the abstract Neo-Expressionism introduced by Hartung and Wols has come to the front; it attempts to record on the

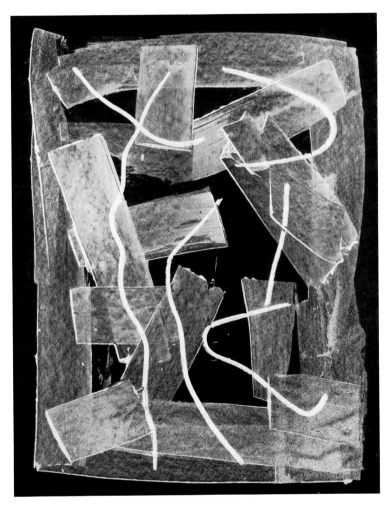

Werner: Premonition (Vorahnung). 1952. Gouache on paper, 35 3/8 × 27 1/2''.
Collection Mrs. Gertrud A. Mellon, New York

canvas surface, in the most spontaneous calligraphy, moments of human consciousness. Many names may be mentioned in this connection: Hann Trier (born 1915), Fred Thieler (born 1916), Hoffmann-Soenderborg (born 1923), Goetz (born 1914), Greis (born 1913), Bernhard Schultze (born 1915), etc. This is a very rich representation of contemporary abstract painting, and it has recapitulated the basic pattern of modern painting in the West.

This exhibition presents three independent, significant personalities who already have a large body of work behind them: Fritz Winter, Theodor Werner, and Ernst Wilhelm Nay. Perhaps they represent the high points of present-day German painting; at any rate, their work certainly shows its characteristic processes.

Fritz Winter (born 1905) most clearly belongs to that fine continuity of German romantic thought that the Blaue Reiter introduced into modern sensibility and that was further developed by Klee's work. Winter started from that point. He himself went through the Bauhaus, was Kandinsky's assistant, and was in close relationship to Klee. There was in addition his own personal experience. In his youth Winter had worked as a miner and there, in the gray glimmer of the rocks, had seen and lived with sunken primeval forms, the imprints of an earlier world. The processes of becoming and passing away here came to life for him in a secret stratum. They summoned him to see creation in the finely formed images of nature, and to understand them more broadly with a view of their hidden processes, to take into consideration not only their nouns: a tree, a stream, a flower, but also their verbs: growing, flowing, blooming. Winter sought a form at the level of the pictorial that could convey this poetic experience. If we closely examine the two pictures by Winter in the exhibition (pages 133-134), we can trace the poetic and constructive intensification of his characteristically romantic feeling for nature. He returns to the point at which man is himself part of creation, and from which "original point of creation," as Klee called it, he repeats ways of becoming and growing which coincide with the processes of all nature. Faced by these pictures, our concepts of objective and abstract break down. We see in them, it is true, non-representational diagrams of physical and psychic energies, structures, fields of force, basic crystalline patterns. But these abstract schemes are permeated by the suggestion of a deeper connection between Winter's personal expressive world and the motivating forces of a living, organic nature, the universal in us and around us.

Theodor Werner (born 1886), who came to abstract painting by way of Cézanne and the Cubists, has comparable aims, but they are still further removed from the objective world. Against a rich background of atmospheric space are set in motion zigzags, curved forms and arabesques, which are alternately delicate and coarse (pages 135 and 137). The painter's concept of the picture is also attuned to his own experience of the world. Werner's intelligence has absorbed the achievements of modern science and its multi-

Werner: 11/56. 1956. Oil and tempera on canvas, $39\,^3/_8 \times 28\,^3/_4''$. Walther Scharf, Oberstdorf/Allgäu

dimensional picture of the universe. Three-dimensional things no longer count there; they have been replaced by structures of an abstract, algebraic nature, oscillations, movements, tensions. "Man who is at a loss in the new space," says Werner, "must go along with these changes emotionally. As a painter he must find forms that conduct this modern existential space into the imaginary and, then and there, locate it in the emotional domains of color forms." Examining Werner's pictures, we see a spirit at work that contemplates a more universal order, going beyond the painter's mastery of nature or pictorial composition. This spirit seeks to relate artistic form to the new spaces of science, and brings us closer to man's newly-found relationship to an expanding universe.

A Latin spirit may perhaps reject the weighting of the construction and décor of the picture with the far-reaching content Winter and Werner seek. It is true that a picture is always a self-contained, concrete fact, but like every other phenomenon it has both

Nay: With the Red and Black Dots. 1954. Oil on canvas, 49 1/4 × 79 1/4". Kunsthalle, Hamburg

surface and depth. Order, form, construction, these lie on the surface; what motivates them rises out of the depths of man himself.

Ernst Wilhelm Nay (born 1902) stands completely apart from this romantic attitude and its concern with content. He has a very special position in modern painting. Originally Nay, whose humanity and passions put him close to Kirchner, was attracted by that artist's hectic, formal hieroglyphics. However he soon translated them into the realm of color, a color of the sharpest and clearest gradations. His colored forms achieved so strong an evocative force that they became capable of mysterious transformations of optical experience, and even of the discovery of far-removed mythical representations. Often one could ask in their presence, as did Mallarmé before Gauguin's work, "How is it possible to combine so much mystery with such vulgar splendor?" But this "vulgar splendor" linking the interaction of complementaries with a glittering chromatic gradation showed Nay's sure, instinctive feeling for the laws of color relationships. At the same time these color constellations reorganized pictorial space, and set it in motion by the serial ordering of the patches of color. The flat pictorial field was formed from a surface moving in time and space. In recent years Nay has removed one layer after another. He eliminated objective emotions, content, psychological factors, and reduced drawing and form to free spots of color. Next he sought to organize these spots into simple geometrical designs until he had arrived at color as the basic essential of form and surface. This contemplative penetration of his medium crystallized into a theory, freeing his creative intelligence from mere instinct and impulse, thereby also excluding a psychological motivation.

Nay's new pictures are graceful, free, and bright, and leave behind all that is dark, anxious, or emotional. They do not express anything other than themselves, that is, anything beyond the pure concrete formations on the surface. His basic task is to create the picture out of color; his basic theme is to energize the surface of his painting by means of color transitions, which take a theme over the colored surface in characteristic counterpoint. The contrapuntal interweaving of these individual color themes and cadences, playing against the orchestrated color of the surface itself, yields the chromatic composition which "is" the picture. These color energies, which were first given expression as varied, amorphous color patches, became solidified in Nay's latest series of paintings into a basic form, namely, the disk (see Dark Melody, page 140). Nay explains the logic of this development as follows: "Movement, represented two-dimensionally by the diagonals of the plane surface, and immobility, represented by verticals and horizontals, in conjunction produce on the flat surface the disk, which transforms the dynamic energy of motion into a latent energy concentrated in the dot." These potential color energies, spreading like musical voices over the surface, create the intricate polyphonic design of the picture.

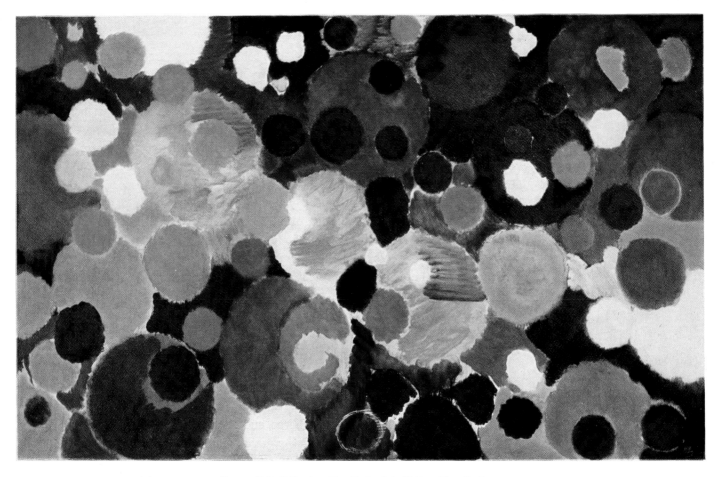

Nay: Dark Melody. 1956. Oil on canvas, 49 $^1/_2$ × 78 $^3/_4$″. Collection Mrs. Gertrud A. Mellon, New York

What we have here is a surprising impulse toward "peinture concrete," which would seem to provide a new direction and a new supply of energy for this particular kind of modern painting. Since the de Stijl contribution of Mondrian and van Doesburg – that is to say about thirty years ago – this painting, despite its basic validity, lapsed into a rigidly monumental platonic geometry. I would not be surprised to find that Nay's paintings, products of pure intuition, alert intelligence, passion, and discipline, may turn out to contain a message that the world would do well to heed. Of his works Nay has said: "They embrace in harmonious relationship, vitality, sentiment, and discipline."

WERNER HAFTMANN

sculpture

German sculpture and painting of our century, like that of earlier periods, has many points of connection with the art of neighboring countries, especially France, and in recent times there has been almost as close a relationship to the art of England and Italy. This association, sometimes tight and sometimes loose, does not, however, have a leveling effect. In the world of form, too, each of the important nations in the field of art possesses its own language and its own development, since in each case the suppositions and traditions have been diverse. It is a fact of German twentieth-century sculpture that despite its manifold interweaving with the sculpture of other nations, it has gone its own way and has its own cachet without being provincial. It is European and German at the same time.

The most important representatives of German sculpture have been known in the United States for a long time, better known than in any other country outside of Germany. Even before World War I, the first works of Georg Kolbe had reached America, and after the war many others followed, thanks especially to the efforts of William R. Valentiner. Gradually a considerable number of the sculptures of Ernst Barlach crossed the Atlantic, and Wilhelm Lehmbruck's art is not represented so impressively in any German museum today as it is in the Museum of Modern Art in New York. The works of these sculptors, like those of the leading contemporary German master Gerhard Marcks, were introduced into the United States principally by Curt Valentin, the art-lover and dealer, who originally came from Germany.

The present exhibition, comprising twenty works of German sculpture covering half a century, can show only some of the main relationships and high points. This historical survey will have to adduce a rather more extensive selection of material in illustrations, in order to fill in at least partially the connecting links between the isolated examples.

The beginning of the new German sculpture is marked by the great figures of Barlach and Lehmbruck. But in order to understand their work and their special contribution in their historical context, it will be well to learn something of the preceding situation of sculpture in Germany.

Around 1900 there were three main official trends in German sculpture, which had a wide impact by reason of the sheer volume of civic monuments and public commissions given out by Kaiser Wilhelm's states and the several other principalities and cities; but the artistic importance of these tendencies is very dubious.

First there was Reinhold Begas (1831-1911) and his school, who filled Berlin and much of the rest of Germany with colossal monuments in a neo-Baroque style of false pathos. A typical example of the formal confusion of the school, and at the same time its "masterpiece" simply because of its size, was the National Monument, completed in 1898, opposite the Berlin Schloss. Then came a new movement in the Secession, connected with the name of Max Klinger (1857-1920), whose pretentious Beethoven Memorial, put together of colored materials, was the subject of passionate esthetic discussion. And finally, there was an effort towards a new monumentality which arose out of the fruitful movement of the Jugendstil. Many good works were created in small sizes, but as soon as the idiom was tested on a monumental scale in large memorials, it showed its emptiness and proved to be merely external, a stylization rather than a style. The Bismarck monument in Hamburg (1906) by Hugo Lederer (1871-1936) is one example, and another is the Battle of the Nations monument near Leipzig (completed in 1913) with statuary by Franz Metzner (1870-1919). These artists are already of the generation of Barlach, who succeeded in crystallizing their vague, formal intentions by endowing them with a meaningful content, and thereby achieved a new style.

We can quickly pass over the official and semi-official artistic tendencies at the turn of the century, but must speak in somewhat more detail of the reappraisal of the true values of sculpture that was produced by the work and, still more, by the writings of Adolph von Hildebrand (1847-1921). His famous book "Das Problem der Form" appeared in 1893 and introduced a new trend toward plasticity. Hildebrand's basic insight and clear conceptions were of decisive importance at the turn of the century for the younger sculptors in Germany who were looking for the way from false pathos to a new lucid formal language. His views were also decisive for German esthetics (as in the case of Heinrich Wölfflin), and they still carry weight today.

In his book Hildebrand drew a sharp distinction between the two main possibilities of sculpture and their effect on style: direct carving and modeling, the creation of form by taking away or by adding.

In his eyes the first was the higher order of work, because he felt that it assured the statue a firm formal and spatial idea, which for him was the essential artistic element of sculpture. Hildebrand believed that sculpture had its origin in drawing, which was then translated into a relief by cutting away in depth and, finally, by a further working loose of the forms, became the free-standing statue.

Consequently, as Hildebrand saw it, the sculptor working in stone or wood must start from a "pictorial idea," which he draws on the face of the stone and then carves out layer by layer. This, of necessity, gives rise to a distinct point of view, according to which all the main saliences must be visible; this he required of any good sculpture.

The modeling technique, building up form from a core, is hazardous, Hildebrand

von Hildebrand: Dionysus. 1890. Marble, $51^1/_4 \times 54^1/_2''$. Collection Mrs. Elisabeth Brewster-Hildebrand, Florence, Italy (*)

believed, because the modeler must continually move around the figure and thereby run the risk of losing a clear pictorial idea. He realized, of course, that artists of strong imagination could produce works which observed his formal principles by using the modeling technique as well. In fact, he himself worked in bronze.

We know today that Hildebrand's theory of direct carving is subject to historical limitations, and that the Greek sculptors to whom he appealed worked all around the figure, cutting it out from all sides at the same time, as practically every modern sculptor does today in either stone or wood. This, however, should not lead us to underestimate his historical importance.

His Youth of 1884 in the National Gallery, Berlin, was conceived as a canon of his theory and had that effect. Because of its strict reference to antique statuary, especially to Augustan Roman, it gives us today the impression of being rather cold. Nevertheless, in the midst of the formal confusion then prevalent, its rigorous, lucid form operated as a liberating force, pointing to a new way. For us his creativeness seems more convincing in the beautiful relief of Dionysus in Florence (above). As a teacher in the

(*) *not in the exhibition*

Munich Academy, Hildebrand trained a succession of students who continued to work in his spirit. He formed a school of sculpture there that kept its unified character even after his death, mainly through his student Hermann Hahn (born 1868). In Munich, too, he created his masterpiece, the Wittelsbach Fountain (1895). Its clear, firm compositon was in contrast to the restless motion of Begas' National Monument in Berlin (1898), and today it still ranks as one of the best civic sculptures of the nineteenth century.

In Berlin he also found followers, in Louis Tuaillon (1862-1919), whose Amazon of 1895 in front of the National Gallery is a fine example of the new style, and in August Gaul (1869-1921). Gaul had derived from the school of Begas, but later in Rome, after contact with Hildebrand and his own study of the antique, he attained new, clear forms; a good example is his bronze lion of 1904 in the Hamburg Kunsthalle (below). With Gaul we have reached the generation of Barlach, whose importance he was one of the first to recognize.

Before proceeding to the artists shown in this exhibition, we must say a few words, at least, to indicate the fructifying and guiding influence of the French sculptors at the turn of the century. This is true in particular of the greatest sculptor of the nineteenth century, Auguste Rodin, both in a positive and negative sense. There is no doubt, for instance, that many of Hildebrand's polemical attacks on the "modeling style" were directed not only against Begas but also against Rodin and his German imitators. Some of Max Klinger's clever, although dangerously formless, bronze busts are inconceivable without Rodin. Younger artists were entirely under Rodin's influence: Karl Albiker (born 1878) was in his studio in 1900, and Georg Kolbe (1877-1947), when still a painter, received decisive impressions from Rodin in Paris in 1898 and became a sculptor as

Gaul: Lion. 1904. Bronze, 52″ high.
Kunsthalle, Hamburg (*)

144

a result of his contact with the Frenchman. Ernesto de Fiori (1884-1945) and Edwin Scharff (1887-1955) similarly found the way from painting to sculpture under Rodin's influence in Paris, during the period between 1911 and the first World War. The German poet Rainer Maria Rilke, at that time Rodin's secretary, wrote his inspired and inspiring biography in 1903; many German lovers of art visited the master in Paris and Meudon, and many of his works reached German private collections and museums. As early as 1898 the National Gallery acquired its first Rodin bust, followed in 1903 by the Age of Brass, and full-sized figures were later collected by many museums in Frankfurt, Leipzig, Bremen, Essen, Munich, etc.

While Rodin's fame was at its height, there came the balancing influence of Aristide Maillol. In 1906 the Berlin Secession exhibited works by Maillol, some of which were also placed in the National Gallery, and other museums and collectors bought and showed his sculpture. In Maillol's art an authentic Mediterranean sensuality gave rise to the classical simplicity and clarity of form that Hildebrand aimed at, but with the important difference that Maillol did not start from the relief or from a pictorial point of view, but modeled in the round from all sides. In their reliefs however the two artists came very close to each other. Maillol was not so much of a theoretician as Hildebrand, but he was a finer artist, and so it is no wonder that in the long run his influence was greater. His impact on sculpture in Germany and in the entire world can be compared only with that of Rodin.

There was still another foreign sculptor of quite a different character who played an important role in the new German sculpture during these years – the Belgian George Minne (1867-1941). Minne's impalpable spirituality is almost the antithesis of Maillol's natural Mediterranean sensuality. But it is important to realize that despite their divergence in style, and the distance separating their native provinces, at the southern and northern limits of the French-speaking regions, both of these significant sculptors derived from the same literary and artistic movement, Symbolism. Maillol, who began as a painter and tapestry-weaver, received his first stylistic impressions from the Nabi group of Symbolist painters: Maurice Denis, Sérusier, Roussel, Bonnard, etc. Minne had been in contact not so much with the painters as with the writers of Symbolism, namely, with his countrymen Emile Verhaeren and Maurice Maeterlinck, whose writings he illustrated. The factor that today still links the two artists in our eyes is a period style of flowing, linear contour, which we in Germany call the Jugendstil, but which originated in France with Gauguin and the Revue Blanche group of Nabis and Symbolists.

Minne had exhibited in Germany earlier than Maillol, appearing repeatedly in the Berlin Secession from 1900, and in 1906 his masterpiece, the fountain for the Folkwang-Museum in Hagen (now in Essen), was erected. The fine-limbed, kneeling boys in the fountain group, with their strongly accented, rhythmic forms, had far-reaching reper-

Minne: Mourning Women. 1896. Wood,
25 $^1/_4$" high. Kunsthalle, Hamburg (*)

cussions in Germany. Still more important as a prototype, however, was a series of
draped figures and groups of figures, such as the Mourning Women of 1896 in the
Hamburg Kunsthalle (above), which recaptured the expressive, medieval language of
draperies. Barlach later went forward from this point.

Ernst Barlach (1870-1938) was only three years younger than Minne, but he achieved
his own style much later than the Belgian artist. Like most of the sculptors of his generation he began as a painter, or rather as a draftsman, and remained a significant graphic
artist all his life. Many of his early drawings which appeared in the magazine Jugend
must convince even those who cannot see the relationship in his mature works, of the
origin of his world of forms in the Jugendstil. At the turn of the century the magazine
was an important center of the movement. Barlach's early drawings also show his
remarkable gifts as a draftsman. On the other hand his early sculpture is so thoroughly
dominated by the conventional forms of the official art of the period that it is much
harder for us to glimpse his mature artistic personality in them than in, for example,

his little textbook, "Figurenzeichnen." Here, along with architectonic designs in the style of Lederer and Metzner, are forms which foreshadow his later work. In the spirit of the Jugendstil, one of whose aims was the revival of applied arts, are Barlach's ceramics, which brought him an appointment as teacher at a school for that craft.

Barlach's characteristic work, which we today consider the beginning of modern German sculpture, began only in 1906 and was stimulated by the experience of a trip to Russia where his brother was working as an engineer. In contrast to the complicated individuals of the present day, the people of the endless Russian plains, who were "alike inwardly and outwardly," became for Barlach simple and, hence, powerful symbolic forms, and they revealed to him a new possibility of plastic creation. Thereafter his forms were directed toward an extreme simplicity and a highly condensed expressive power, and his figures became archtypes of spiritual conditions: Beggar Woman (or as it might better be known, Poverty), Sorrowing Woman (or better, Sorrow), The Avenger, The Solitary, etc.

One cannot comprehend the specific nature of Barlach's art without realizing that he was also an important poet and, above all, a writer of drama. The characters in his plays are analogous to the characters in his sculpture. In his poems too there prevails a heavy, often tendentious seriousness, a tragic undertone that characterizes all of his work. Here and there is some grim humor, but never gaiety.

His first works after the trip to Russia are in clay, some of which were intended for firing in porcelain, or for bronze casting. An example is the expressive Beggar Woman of 1907 (below) which goes back to a sketch out of his book, "Figurenzeichnen," but

Barlach: Beggar Woman. 1907. Bronze, 9" high.
Collection Hermann Reemtsma, Hamburg (*)

147

Barlach: Sorrowing Woman. 1909. Wood, 26″ high.
Present whereabouts unknown (*)

which has achieved an independent plastic form for the first time. Depersonalization is carried so far in this figure that apart from the hands nothing recognizable is left of the body, and only the drapery gives voice to the expression. Draped figures, in the sense in which Minne had rediscovered them, now became and remained Barlach's unique and solitary theme. Not a single nude figure came from his hand, surely the only such case in European sculpture since the Middle Ages.

Barlach soon discovered the material that was best suited for his world of forms: wood. Since the end of the Baroque period wood had been rarely used and then only for works below the first rank. The revival was not due to Barlach alone. Gauguin had preceded him, and Maillol had followed him in some early works. The most immediate source of inspiration for Barlach in this connection, however, was Minne.

Such works of sculpture in wood as the Sorrowing Woman of 1909 (above) bring out with special clarity the extent to which Hildebrand's basic pictorial rules still held validity for Barlach, despite the divergence of the two artists in spirit and expression. Barlach, the draftsman, also starts from a "pictorial idea," cuts one layer after another out of the wood, moving from front to back, so that it is quite natural for all the forms

148

Barlach: Man in Stocks. 1918. Wood,
28 3/4" high. Kunsthalle, Hamburg

to be seen from a single point of view. The backs of the figures are, to be sure, given form, but they are not essential to the expression. Barlach's figures are thought of as standing against the wall, and for that reason he was also able to create architectural sculpture.

Another characteristic of Barlach's style is the utter self-containment of his closed forms. The draperies unify the bodies into a monolithic block, and the arms are close to the body or concealed by the drapery. Only rarely, and then usually in bronzes such as the Singing Man of 1928 (page 152), did he abandon this principle. In general his formal elements are reduced to the opposition between concave and convex. Occasionally, as in the Man in Stocks of 1918 (page 149), the darkness of a deep incision comes to eloquent expression. These self-contained blocks are for the most part in a state of heavy repose, sitting, lying, standing, sometimes gently rocking. There are, however, exceptions which express violent movement and great emotional excitement. A marked example of this is The Avenger of 1922 (opposite).

Barlach's first works in the new style soon found a response among the more perceptive lovers of art. Of special significance for him was the friendship of August Gaul, who recognized his importance and introduced him to Paul Cassirer, the art dealer. This enabled him to move in 1910 to the small city of Güstrow in Mecklenburg, where he worked in seclusion until his death. It need hardly be said that his art at the beginning was completely rejected by the public, and the antagonism to his work persisted even when, after the first World War, it had made its way into the museums. Indeed this hostility even increased when some adventurous municipalities commissioned him to create war memorials which, of course, were entirely outside the conventions of traditional sculpture and showed no traces of the "heroic," fortunately. Barlach created four memorials: in 1927, the Hovering Angel in the church at Güstrow (page 155); in 1928 the Fighter of the Spirit (page 153) at Kiel, honoring the dead soldiers from the university; in 1929 for the cathedral in Magdeburg the great wooden group of three soldiers behind the cemetery cross, in front of which the graves are opening; and in 1931 the great simple stele in Hamburg with the relief of a mourning mother and child. All these monuments, which are Barlach's most magnificent achievements, were removed during the Third Reich, but it was possible to set all of them up again after the war. The same fate befell the important series of figures commissioned for the façade of St. Catherine's Church in Lübeck; by 1933 he had succeeded in completing three of these huge, impressive figures, and two casts of each were made in glazed ceramic, one for the church (page 154), and one to be sold in order to finance the whole scheme. The Busch-Reisinger Museum in Cambridge, Massachusetts has the Beggar from this series. The figures could be installed in Lübeck for the first time only after the war; the six missing ones were made by Gerhard Marcks.

150

Barlach: The Avenger. 1922. Wood, 24″ high. Collection Herman Shulman, New York

Barlach: Singing Man. 1928. Bronze, 19 $^1/_2$″ high. The Museum of Modern Art, New York, Mrs. John D. Rockefeller, Jr. Fund

Barlach: The Fighter of the Spirit (Der Geistkämpfer).
1928. Bronze, 18′ high. Memorial for fallen students
of Kiel University (*)

Barlach's significance in modern German sculpture consists primarily in the discovery of completely simple, elementary means and in the absolute honesty of the deeply-felt, new sensous content.

Alongside Barlach, at the fountainhead of modern German sculpture, stands Wilhelm Lehmbruck, Barlach's antithesis spiritually, artistically, in his personal origins, and the sources of his art. The appearance of two such different artists on the scene was an extraordinary piece of good fortune for German art, forestalling the danger of one-sidedness which might well have occurred if only one of these two strong personalities had been present in a single period.

opposite, Barlach: Hovering Angel (Schwebender Engel). 1927. Bronze, 8' long. Memorial in the Cathedral in Güstrow. (Second cast for St. Anthony Church, Cologne, illustrated) (*)

Barlach: Woman in the Wind (Die Frau im Wind). 1932. Glazed ceramic, 6' 6³/₄" high. Façade of St. Catherine's Church, Lübeck (*)

Lehmbruck (1880-1919) was ten years younger than Barlach. The older man had come from Wedel in Holstein near Hamburg, and he was conditioned by the North German character. Lehmbruck, on the other hand, was born in Meiderich near Duisburg in the West. The son of a miner, he took up sculpture at the nearby academy of Düsseldorf and then went to Paris, where he received his formative impulses. Barlach had found nothing in the French capital that he could take away with him. The West German Lehmbruck had a much more European attitude from the outset. But as we observe the two artists from our vantage point in time, which gives us a perspective on the artistically significant years before the first World War, we can find a deep inner relationship in the tragic sense of life they shared. In both cases it stemmed from the dolorous rejection of a world fallen prey to externality, materialism, and hastening catastrophe.

As early as 1907 Lehmbruck had exhibited his group, Mother and Child, in the Paris Salon and had also made several trips from Düsseldorf to the French capital. He lived in Paris from 1910 to 1914, and there his early masterpieces were created in a sudden rise of inspiration. The first is the great Standing Woman of 1910 (opposite); it is far more impressive than anything he had hitherto done and remains today one of the most important works of twentieth-century German sculpture. It has been said that contact with Maillol's work released new powers in him. This is certainly not entirely false but is still only part of the truth. For even though the simplification of the forms and the clear organization of the whole are close to Maillol's treatment of form, Lehmbruck's melancholy expression is completely alien to the bright affirmative nature of the southern Frenchman. Similar echoes are apparent in Lehmbruck's early work, and we know both from personal statements and our own visual experience, that this is the result of the influence of Hans von Marées (1837-1887), the great painter who is far too little known outside of Germany. Marées had been a friend of Hildebrand, and many of Hildebrand's thoughts came originally from him. Lehmbruck goes back directly to Marées and succeeds in giving a sculptural embodiment to the painter's pictorial and formal ideas.

But what Marées tried all his life to express in pictorial form was only a phase for Lehmbruck. In the next year, 1911, he created the Kneeling Woman (page 159), a tremendous step into new territory which at first threw even Lehmbruck's friends into confusion. On the basis of recent research we know Lehmbruck met Brancusi that year and visited him in his studio. It is also probable that he met Modigliani at the same time through Brancusi. But this does not explain the change. It may be that Brancusi gave him the courage to undertake bold steps in form, and that Modigliani had a corresponding melancholy, but what Lehmbruck created here is entirely his own. The reminiscences of Marées have vanished. We see excessively slim limbs, unnaturally attenuated in a wonderfully harmonious melody of contour and soft, melancholy expressions;

Lehmbruck: Standing Woman. 1910. Bronze (cast in 1916-17),
6′ 4″ high. City Art Museum of St. Louis, Missouri

Lehmbruck: Kneeling Woman. 1911.
Cast stone, 69 $^1/_2''$ high.
The Museum of Modern Art, New York,
Mrs. John D. Rockefeller, Jr. Fund

Lehmbruck: Bowing Female Torso. 1913. Terra cotta,
35 $^1/_2''$ high. Collection Mr. and Mrs. Morton D. May,
St. Louis, Missouri

his forms are not active like Barlach's but abandoned to a mood. Barlach was a dramatist, whereas Lehmbruck was a lyricist. And in point of fact, he wrote some beautiful lyric poems.

Two years later, in 1913, came the Bowing Female Torso (above) and the Standing Youth (page 161). A noteworthy feature of the latter is the further attenuation of the limbs, and even more clearly than in the Kneeling Woman, we feel the emphatic axes of the body, which are filled with a spiritual, expressive power. The fact that nature is radically transformed here gives rise to new possibilities of artistic expression. These were the years of the birth of Cubism and of abstract art (with Kandinsky, in Munich). Lehmbruck did not go so far and, for all his distortions and transformations, remained close to nature. Today his works seem almost classical to us.

158

In 1914 the war forced him to return to Germany; he lived first in Berlin, in Zurich from 1917 on and, after the war, in Berlin again. The meaningless blood-baths of the war had depressed him deeply. Many of his poems of the period already express the wish to die. The sculptures of these late years utter the same message. The Seated Youth (below) of 1918 is so much a "mourning figure" that between the wars it convincingly served in Lehmbruck's native city as a symbolic figure for a war cemetery – until the National Socialists removed it. But along with its emotional power, it reveals new artistic methods and possibilities. The space enclosed by the limbs becomes a hollow, and the hollow form becomes a determining element of the artistic form. This is the rudimentary starting point for new formal departures which were to be further developed in modern German sculpture. Outside of Germany Henry Moore has gone forward most decisively in this direction.

Lehmbruck himself could no longer endure life. Just as he began to have some success in Germany, and after he had become a member of the Prussian Academy of Art in Berlin, and the National Gallery and other German museums had acquired his sculpture, he took his own life. The work of his maturity, which seems to us today to

opposite, Lehmbruck: Standing Youth. 1913. Cast stone, 7′ 8″ high. The Museum of Modern Art, New York, gift of Mrs. John D. Rockefeller, Jr.

Lehmbruck: Seated Youth. 1918. Cast stone 41$^{1}/_{2}$″ high. Kunstmuseum, Duisburg (*)

left, Kolbe: Dancer. 1911-12. Bronze, 60 $^1/_2$″ high. National Gallery, Berlin (*). *center,* de Fiori: Youth. 1911. Bronze, 43 $^1/_4$″ high. Kunsthalle, Mannheim (*). *right,* Albiker: Youth. 1911. Bronze, 28 $^3/_8$″ high. Folkwang Museum, Essen (*)

Kolbe: Assunta. 1921. Bronze, 6' 3" high.
The Detroit Institute of Arts, Detroit,
Michigan

be the greatest achievement of German sculpture in the twentieth century, was created in the short period of nine years.

Barlach and Lehmbruck are the only two important sculptors whose work has anything to do with the much misused and misinterpreted concept of Expressionism. At any rate, both of them sought to heighten expression by new artistic means, and both drew upon an inner vision. What they began was to be taken up and carried forward by a younger generation. Those who were closer to them in age partially realized their importance, but traveled different ways.

Lehmbruck's generation in Germany was extraordinarily rich in talented sculptors, not all of whom can be mentioned here. Georg Kolbe (1877-1947), who is represented by one work in the exhibition, was the most famous of them. However mention should also be made of at least a few of his contemporaries. In order to bring out clearly the differences between the earnest new language of Lehmbruck and the traits held in common by his contemporaries, we give here illustrations of three works dated 1911, the year of Lehmbruck's Kneeling Woman: Kolbe's Dancer in the Berlin National Gallery, Ernesto de Fiori's Youth in the Mannheim Kunsthalle, and Karl Albiker's Youth in the Folkwang Museum, Essen (opposite). When we examine them retrospectively, it is astonishing how uniform in effect are the styles of these three artists, however different their origins. Their figures are fixed in the movements of the dance. They represent a moment in time arrested by the artist, rather than the timeless, unchanging aspect of things which was captured in the sculpture of both Barlach and Lehmbruck.

Karl Albiker (born 1878) was with Rodin around 1900. He is the only one of the group who began directly as a sculptor and not as a painter. Ernesto de Fiori (1884-1945) was born in Rome and was half-Italian, but his artistic development belongs entirely to German art. After studying painting in Munich, he lived in Paris between 1911 and 1914, and there for the first time became a sculptor, also under Rodin's influence. The same artistic origin is seen in the early works of Georg Kolbe which precede the Dancer. All three sculptures above are early productions by artists who created rich and many-sided bodies of work, but their characteristic styles are revealed in these early works and remain the same, despite an increasing mastery and a change in the formulations of their sculptural problems. Georg Kolbe was the only one who, in the years after the first World War when Expressionism was victorious everywhere in Germany, transformed his style into a strict and rigorous formalism. One of the most important examples of this period is his Assunta of 1921 (left) which was brought to Detroit by Kolbe's friend and biographer, William R. Valentiner. Here the form is clearer, more simplified, and rhythmical than in either earlier or later works, for Kolbe soon went back to his first dancer themes.

Some younger sculptors went further along similar paths. The most important of this group is Edwin Scharff (1887-1955), who also began as a painter, was in Paris from 1911 to 1914 with Lehmbruck, Fiori, and others, and there became a sculptor under the combined influence of Rodin and Maillol. The strict rhythms of his first great sculpture, the Athlete of 1913, already show his great gift. Later at the Berlin Academy, Scharff was a remarkable teacher of the younger generation, especially of Mettel and Blumenthal. His Torso of 1932 (below) in the Hamburg Kunsthalle dates from this period; despite its sensuousness, it reveals possibilities of a heightened abstraction.

The sculptor Renée Sintenis (born 1888) was even more faithful to the Impressionist form. The charming little animal figures for which she is primarily known are characterized by instantaneous movement and restless surfaces. She has done only a few larger works, the most important of which is Daphne of 1930 (opposite): an especially slender form with arms flung high, seized at the moment that she turns herself into a tree in order to escape the pursuing Apollo. There is as yet no explicit Surrealist statement, and room is left for the observer's fancy.

These sculptors, and many others who could have been mentioned, were still basically impressionistic, seeking to reproduce instantaneous movement and relying on the seduction of the surface. Certainly they do not belong to the avant garde, and their

Scharff: Torso. 1932. Bronze, 43 $^{1}/_{4}$″ high. Kunsthalle, Hamburg (*)

Sintenis: Daphne. 1930. Bronze, 56 1/2″ high. The Museum of Modern Art, New York, Mrs. John D. Rockefeller, Jr. Fund

historical importance is far below that of Barlach and Lehmbruck. It can be said of Kolbe, for example, that although he was successful all his life and was considered by many to be the leading German sculptor of his time, his influence ended with his death. However we cannot ignore the historical function of this belated Impressionist sculpture. Thanks to its appearance and thanks also to its general recognition, it succeeded in doing away with the sculpture of false pathos and empty monumentality which had previously dominated official artistic life. Although this art may not be timeless and was not to leave its stamp on the future, it was beyond any doubt art for art's sake and thereby had a purifying effect.

Victory over Impressionist form in German sculpture was achieved by a number of sculptors who followed Barlach and Lehmbruck and were more or less the contemporaries of the younger artists mentioned above, producing their decisive works after the first World War. Only some of the most important names can be mentioned here: Gustav H. Wolff (1886-1934), Gerhard Marcks (born 1889), Toni Stadler (born 1888), Philipp Harth (born 1887), Ewald Mataré (born 1887), Herbert Garbe (1888-1946), Rudolf Belling (born 1886), Emy Roeder (born 1890), Richard Haizmann (born 1895). Only four of these are represented in the exhibition. One general remark can be made which applies to all of them: the purpose of their art is no longer, as it was in the case of Kolbe, the representation of life, but rather the creation of the sculpture itself, the plastic work of stone, bronze, or wood. This may seem obvious, but it is the essence of their position. Their starting point is a different one, and their new attitude to the work opened the way to a free transformation of the visible world, to abstraction, indeed, to non-objective forms. While it is true that the development proceded more slowly than it did in France, it was a genuine development, independent and organic. Stimuli from the outside were received and assimilated, but new directions were not widely embraced. German sculpture of this generation was not without self-consciousness.

Gustav H. Wolff, highly gifted, stubborn, self-taught, was both painter and sculptor as well as a writer. His early death truncated his work, but his forceful sculpture has had broad influence. In 1925 he made two life-size figures for a private house in Hamburg which were to be on either side of a fireplace, but which never reached the place designated for them. We illustrate the female figure which was to go at the left (page 167). Its vigorous simplifications and almost crude shapes maintain the essential quality of stone. A rigorous frontality, which is the necessary aspect of architectural sculpture, still thoroughly satisfies Hildebrand's requirements although the style is far removed from the classicism of the great theoretician. The simplicity of Wolff's formal idiom is rather in Barlach's tradition. The extent to which Gerhard Marcks later followed Wolff's path is seen by comparing Wolff's sculpture with Marcks' Shenandoah of 1932 and with the great Mourning Angel of 1946-49 (page 167), erected in Cologne as a

Wolff: Portrait of the Poet Gottfried Benn. 1927.
Clay, 12¼″ high. Kunsthalle, Hamburg (*)

memorial to the victims of the bombings. Wolff's work showed a wealth of formal possibilities. His portrait head of the poet Gottfried Benn of 1927 (above) was freely formed in clay and then fired, and because of the nature of the materials, the form is round and suggests work in ceramics. The translation of the individual into the typical is reminiscent of late Roman portraits.

The work of Gerhard Marcks, which today continues to develop in a broad stream, is especially rich in form and spiritual content. His work embraces tender grace along with the grotesque, a quiet, self-contained intimacy, and great monumental form. The paths struck out by Barlach and Lehmbruck unite in him in a new style, and his influence, in turn, extends over the entire artistic scene in Germany. Each of the artists contemporary with him or younger has had to reckon with his work. He is still today the center of German sculpture.

The animal sculpture which he created before 1914 in the tradition of August Gaul was not pursued after 1918. Marcks went to the Bauhaus in Weimar where he took over the Dornburg ceramics studio. Along with this craft activity he produced new archaistic sculptures in which he reacted to the challenging style of Oskar Schlemmer's paintings. When the Bauhaus moved to Dessau, Marcks went to the Kunstschule in Halle, quietly continuing his work. A trip to Greece in 1928 confirmed his own direction and brought him new strength. From 1933 to the end of the second World War he lived again in his native Berlin, whose sculptural tradition is still alive in many aspects of his work. In

166

left, Wolff: Standing Woman. 1925. Stone figure for a mantel, 82 1/4″ high. Kunsthalle, Hamburg (*). *center,* Marcks: Shenandoah. 1932. Stone, 68 3/4 high. Destroyed (*). *right,* Marcks: Mourning Angel. 1946-49. Stone, 8′ 6 1/4″ high. Memorial for the dead of World War II, Cologne (*)

167

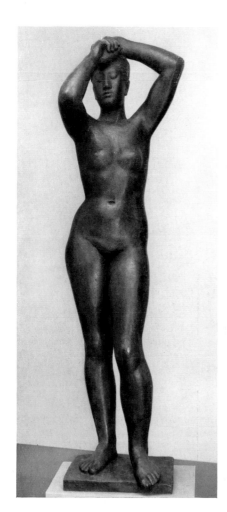

left, Marcks: Maja. 1942. Bronze, 89″ high. Collection Nelson A. Rockefeller, New York.
right, Marcks: Melusine III. 1949. Bronze, 43 $^1/_2$″ high. Walker Art Center, Minneapolis, Minnesota

Marcks: Albertus Magnus. 1955. Bronze, 8′ 10$^1/_4$″ high. University of Cologne (*)

left, Stadler: Standing Girl. 1935-38. Cast stone, 66 $^1/_8$″ high. Kunsthalle, Hamburg (*)

right, Stadler: Diver (Taucher). 1953. Bronze, 45 $^1/_4$″ high. Owned by the artist (*)

particular, Gottfried Schadow (1764-1850) has always been a model and a guide for him. G. H. Wolff was then still living in Berlin, and there Marcks met other contemporaries and a number of younger sculptors: Toni Stadler, Philipp Harth, Ludwig Kasper, Hermann Blumenthal, Hans Mettel, and others. He became the center of this group. Curt Valentin, who was then operating the Buchholz-Galerie in Berlin, was the dealer and personal friend of all these artists. The Berlin years were very fruitful for Marcks despite the ruinous official artistic policies that soon made any exhibition or public appearance impossible. In a work like Kastalia, 1933, the block-like fullness of Barlach is combined with the lyrical expressiveness of Lehmbruck, and this synthesis remained a permanent one. After the war when, along with Edwin Scharff, he was called to the Hochschule in Hamburg as a teacher, he completed Barlach's series of figures for St. Catherine's Church in Lübeck, tactfully taking on the style of the older man and translating it into his own quieter forms. At the same time he produced major works such as a memorial in Hamburg and the Mourning Angel in Cologne. Since 1950 he has been living in Cologne where he recently completed for the university the magnificent monument to Albertus Magnus, the medieval scholastic (page 169).

Toni Stadler (born 1888) played in Munich a role similar to that of Marcks in Berlin. The tradition of Hildebrand was especially alive in Munich, and in the period between the wars Hildebrand's disciple, Hermann Hahn (born 1870), and his followers dominated sculpture there. Stadler had passed under the influence of this school, after having been

Stadler: Dog. 1950. Bronze, 40 $^1/_2''$ high.
Bayerische Staatsgemäldesammlungen, Munich

previously with Gaul in Berlin. But he succeeded in overcoming its limitations. Disciplined by archaic Greek and Etruscan works, his style worked itself free from a strict pictorial idea and acquired breadth once again. A group of friends followed him stylistically: Anton Hiller (born 1893), Georg Brenninger (born 1909), Heinrich Kirchner (born 1902). It was only after the war that the work of Marino Marini appeared, confirming Stadler's course. The fact is that Munich has always been artistically closer to Italy than Berlin has been. In Munich Barlach seemed far removed from local artistic interests, and at best only the early work of Lehmbruck had any effect. Stadler's Standing Girl, 1935-38 (page 170) in the Hamburg Kunsthalle, intimates this relationship to Lehmbruck; the Dog, 1950 (page 171) shows Stadler's great plastic power and also indicates his complete liberation from the school of Hildebrand.

The contribution of Philipp Harth (born 1887), who has written penetrating articles on sculptural creation, is not so much a liberation from Hildebrand's theory as a more fruitful extension of it. Like that of August Gaul, his sculpture has been confined almost exclusively to animals in wood, stone, bronze, and occasionally in copper. His intention is to gain clear visibility for a piece of sculpture, not from one side as in Hildebrand, but from all sides, forming it in such a way that all the essential plastic forms can be sensed from any angle of vision. His Jaguar, 1928, in wood (below) is a good example of this, and also shows how the closed form of the wooden block is retained. All Harth's works represent the animal in a typical attitude; they are not always so close to nature as the Jaguar, but the exact study of nature is the basis of his formal world.

left, Harth: Jaguar. 1928. Wood, 29^1/$_2$'' high. National Gallery, Berlin (*). right, Mataré: Young Bull. 1923. Wood, 18^1/$_2$ × 24^3/$_4$''. Saarland Museum, Saarbrücken

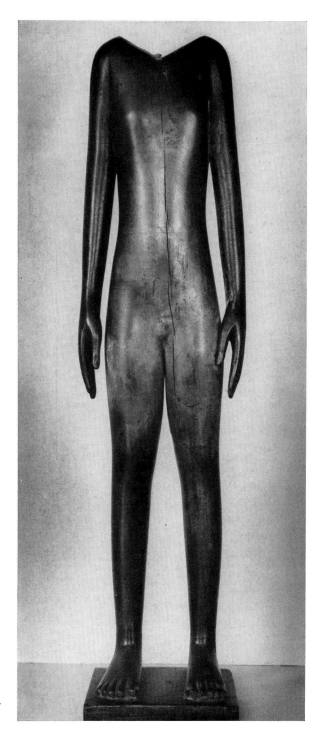

Mataré: Standing Figure. 1926-27. Walnut, 21⁵/₈″ high.
Collection Dr. Hugo Häring, Biberach an der Riss

Belling: Sculpture. 1923. Bronze, partly silvered, $18^7/_8''$ high.
The Museum of Modern Art, New York, A. Conger Goodyear Fund

A contemporary of his from the Rhineland is Ewald Mataré (born 1887), whose early work is also to a great extent animal portrayal. However he goes about it in an entirely different manner: he does not start from nature but from simple, self-contained, basic forms, out of which the animal figure grows. His works have a much more generalized effect because he starts with abstract form and then succeeds in bringing to immediate expression such qualities as the tense lurking of a cat, and the dull heaviness of a bull (page 172). The beauty of the material plays an important role for Mataré. He makes conscious use of the grain of the wood and the pattern of the bronze as artistic means, and in order to bring them to full effectiveness all detailed forms are removed. With such an approach it was natural that he should also have made many objects in various craft media: intarsia, ceramics, and stained glass. His beautiful colored woodcuts go perhaps even further in the creation of simplified symbols than do his sculptural works.

After the second World War he executed many important commissions, including the bronze doors for the Cologne Cathedral. In these impressive works, in which bronze relief and mosaic are combined, the basic forms of his early sculpture are supplemented by reminiscences of Romanesque art.

Rudolf Belling of Berlin (born 1886) took another route to abstraction. He sought a new relationship between sculpture and architecture, and collaborated successfully on many occasions with German and Dutch architects. His aim was a precision of form which he carried to the point of a machine-like quality. This is not very apparent in his first completely non-objective works, such as the Triad of 1919 in the National Gallery. Expressionistic elements are still present, as they are in the early abstract works of his contemporary Herbert Garbe, done in the same period. It is also important to realize that the Russian Alexander Archipenko, who was the same age as Belling, had a powerful influence in Germany at the beginning of the century. His first one-man show was held in 1910 at the Folkwang Museum in Hagen, and after the war his work was shown repeatedly in Berlin where he lived from 1921 to 1923 before going to the United States. Many of his sculptures entered German museums and private collections, and these certainly influenced Belling. The work of Brancusi was also well known in Germany at that time. Nevertheless, it may be said that a work such as Belling's Sculp-

Haizmann: Eagle. 1931. Polished bronze, 26 ³/₄″. Collection Dr. Guhr, Hamburg (*)

ture, 1923, (page 174) in the Museum of Modern Art, which seems exclusively to emphasize a machine-like precision, first tested the possibilities of the simultaneous operation of inner and outer forms which Henry Moore developed only much later (in The Helmet) and on the basis of entirely different premises. The application of polished materials of different colors – brass and silver – was later taken up and varied by Hans Uhlmann. Belling left Germany in 1933 and is living today in Istanbul, where he has created more conventional sculptures.

A younger, extremely individualistic, self-taught sculptor, Richard Haizmann (born 1895), worked in a similar direction quite independently of Mataré or Belling, and developed still further their simplified basic forms. On occasion he, too, like Brancusi or Belling, polished the surface of bronze or brass to a mirror-like finish, and he has also created completely non-objective works. His masterpiece in polished bronze, the Eagle of 1931 (page 175), erects a free idea of form into a symbol that renounces all outward representation but still possesses something of the eagle. The work was created as a sketch for a war monument in Hamburg which was later executed by Barlach.

Haizmann was an art dealer before he began to work as an artist around 1927. In addition to his sculpture he has done ceramics with interesting new forms, and also drawings and lithographs. Between the wars he was a major force in the artistic life of Hamburg. His work is almost forgotten today, but unjustly so. Since the war he has moved along other paths, but the possibilities that he was the first to investigate still continue to live in younger artists such as Karl Hartung. He undoubtedly knew some works of Brancusi, and Archipenko, too, may have had a liberating effect on him, but his work occupies an independent place between the two generations.

Since Haizmann's work attracted little attention outside of Hamburg, despite the energetic advocacy of Max Sauerlandt, the art historian, it is quite possible that such an artist as Otto Baum (born 1900) hardly knew of him at the time he began to work. Baum, who was a machinist and a sailor during the first World War, became interested in sculpture as a student in the Stuttgart Academy in 1924. After interesting experiments with the human form, which he subjected occasionally to bold distortions, he returned, like Haizmann, principally to the representation of animals. These he constructed from basic plastic shapes (above) in an effort to grasp what is typical in the animal.

The only German sculptor of this generation who has worked continuously and with consistent logic in purely non-objective forms is Hans Uhlmann (born 1900). From the character of his works it seems perfectly natural that, after some beginnings in sculpture in 1925, he should have attended the Technische Hochschule in Berlin and studied engineering. (It is interesting to note that the American Alexander Calder, who was two years his senior, had also been an engineering student.) During his period of study Uhlmann also taught at the Technische Hochschule, but this came to an end in 1933. His

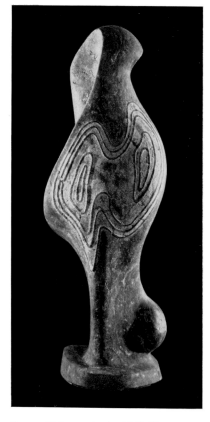

Baum: Metamorphosis. 1948-49. Limestone, $39\,^3/_8''$ high. Owned by the artist

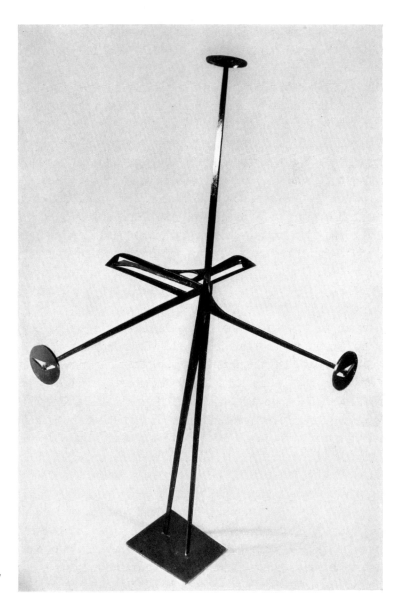

Uhlmann: Construction. 1954. Steel,
63″ high. Owned by the artist

sculptural activity went forward at the same time, fertilized by the newly-won technical procedures. In 1930 he exhibited for the first time but attracted little attention. During a period of artistic seclusion between 1933 and 1945, his powers ripened, and when in 1947 he once again showed a group of his works, he immediately won an assured place in the development of modern German sculpture. Since 1950 he has been a professor at the Berlin Academy. He has done a series of massive, plastic forms cast in bronze, dating from the end of the forties, whose sharp-edged, chiseled shapes contain echoes of human forms. Since that time, however, he has been making free, symbolic constructions from the most diverse technical material, brass wire, steel pipe, strip steel, etc., with an astonishing richness of formal invention which is also visible in his drawings. His technical constructions, worked out with a craftsman's care and precision, articulate the space that they penetrate or encompass with assurance and clarity. They are, therefore, extremely convincing when adapted to modern buildings.

A number of new artists are pursuing the possibilities opened up by Uhlmann's experiments. The younger generation is, of course, also influenced by such non-German artists as Gonzalez or Lardera, who have done work in the same or similar directions. But within his own generation Uhlmann, like Haizmann and Baum, each in a different manner, is alone in Germany. The rest of the German sculptors born between 1900 and 1910 persist in the representation of the human form and are more conservative than their contemporaries in France and England. This does not however diminish their importance. The situation in Germany resembles that of Italy, where the generation that includes Marini (born 1901), Manzù (born 1908), and Fazzini (born 1913) similarly preserve the human form. It would also be completely erroneous to infer that these German artists were affected in their styles by the artistic dictatorship of the Third Reich. Not only were they all rejected by the rulers of that period and prohibited from exhibiting, but all of them, as students of the older generation, had worked out their own styles long before 1933. They had studied Barlach or Lehmbruck or both, and received their formative stimuli from Marcks and Stadler. Their number is surprisingly large and their creativity rich. They are today decisive in the picture of German sculpture. We shall name only a few: Heinrich Kirchner (born 1902), Hans Mettel (born 1903), Hermann Blumenthal (1905-1942), Kurt Lehmann (born 1905), Gustav Seitz (born 1906), Hans Wimmer (born 1907), Georg Brenninger (born 1909). This group is represented by only one work in the exhibition, the Kneeling Youth, 1929-30, of Hermann Blumenthal (opposite). We know today that Blumenthal was the most important sculptor of his generation in Germany, and his early death in the war in Russia was a major loss. Blumenthal came from Essen and was the son of a miner, like his great compatriot Lehmbruck (and Henry Moore, too, for that matter). Before going to the Academy he learned the craft of the stone mason, as did his contemporary Mettel. In Berlin he was

Blumenthal: Kneeling Youth. 1929-30. Bronze, 40 1/2″ high. Ehemals Staatliche Museen Berlin, National Gallery, on loan from the Kulturkreis im Bundesverband der deutschen Industrie

left, Blumenthal: Standing Figure. 1936-37. Bronze, 75″ high. Niedersächsische Landesgalerie, Hanover (*). *center,* Kirchner: Wanderer. 1950. Bronze, 25 $^1/_2$″ high. Owned by the artist (*). *right,* Mettel: Man with Horse. 1950. Bronze, 16 $^1/_8$″ high. Kunsthalle, Hamburg (*)

a student of Edwin Scharff. The softly modeled surfaces of his early reliefs show the influence of his teacher. But Scharff allowed his students freedom and helped them to develop their own powers. Blumenthal soon found his own style and his own expression. The Kneeling Youth, done at the age of twenty-four, is one of his early convincing master-pieces. The influence of Lehmbruck can be noted in the lengthened limbs, but the expression of movement is much more pronounced. There are few figures that animate space so masterfully. During these years, while still a master student at the Academy, he created a series of masculine forms equally powerful in movement. Around 1934 after a first stay in Rome, he produced unrelieved, closed columnar figures, like the Man with Cape (Prodigal Son), in which a very freely-altered Barlach influence can be discerned. Later his style loosened to a free classical form, as in the Standing Figure (above) completed during his second stay in Rome. Once again Blumenthal gives

Hartung: Torso. 1950. 55″ high. Collection
Andrew P. Fuller, Fort Worth, Texas

Heiliger: Head of Ernst Reuter. 1954. Bronze, 18″ high.
Collection Kurt H. Grunebaum, Harrison, New York

us the image of an idealistic youth, in many cases with bound hands, a symbol of an aspiring young man constrained by circumstances. He himself resembled this figure in that, on his way to new heights, he was taken into the army and did not return from the battlefield.

Hans Mettel is two years older than Blumenthal and comes from North Germany. He started from a similar background: apprenticeship as a stone mason, Scharff's school, and Rome. He is more dogged and works more slowly, but his ideas are closely related to Blumenthal's. Many of his works give the impression of being continuations of the road Blumenthal took. They are perhaps even more rigorous and renounce more consciously anything that could be called charm, but they possess great plastic power and a brevity of artistic idea. His feeling for spatial organization is demonstrated by his group, Man with Horse (page 180): the feet, forming six points, are arranged on the base to establish a fixed spatial form. In recent years he has done primarily architectural sculpture. Heinrich Kirchner belongs to the group of friends of Toni Stadler, and his art shows the Munich influence. The bridge from him to Marini, who is about the same age, is easily crossed, but his direction was found quite independently, and the content of his art is remote from that of the Italian. Marini's mounted figures are pagan in spirit, while Kirchner's subjects, such as the Pieta and the Good Shepherd, belong to the Catholic world. His Wanderer (page 180) can be placed between the two trends; it is a primeval man of the forest, formed with great plastic simplicity.

The same generation has brought new experimental possibilities to the front in Germany. As an example there is Karl Hartung (born 1908), who is active today as professor at the Berlin Academy and is one of the strongest of contemporary artistic personalities. Hartung is from Hamburg and undoubtedly received stimulation from Haizmann in his youth. He developed this influence in a fruitful and many-sided manner in his own distinct style. His work combines what seem to be completely contrary tendencies, namely, the abstract and the figurative; and occasionally he even does portraits. Hartung's work, like that of many present-day painters, shows that the contradiction between abstract and objective forms voiced by many critics is no true contradiction, but that the same scheme of values and the same expressive powers may be present in either alternative. A single artist may master both trends without renouncing his own characteristic idiom or his own nature. Hartung's Torso (page 181) may be read, if one wishes, as an echo of the organic human form or as a freely invented form. In any case it is a pure, harmonious sculpture, a pleasure both to the eye and to the touch.

Bernhard Heiliger (born 1915) is the youngest of the sculptors represented in this exhibition. He comes from Stettin where he was a student of an excellent sculptor, Kurt Schwerdtfeger. In Berlin he first oriented himself to Gerhard Marcks and later came very close to Henry Moore, as he sought new forms. In his work, too, the alternatives of the non-objective and figurative coexist. Such portraits as that of the Mayor of Berlin, Dr. Ernst Reuter (opposite), are interesting formally and are also extremely good likenesses.

German sculpture of the twentieth century, which is illustrated in this exhibition by a few chosen examples ranging from Barlach to Hartung, made a not inconsiderable contribution to European art. Its influence outside of Germany is, to be sure, with the single exception of Lehmbruck, less extensive than that of other countries, if we think of Maillol or Moore or Marini. But as a whole it has shown certain unified characteristics, easier to feel than to define, a tendency which promises to endure.

ALFRED HENTZEN

Corinth: Apocalypse. c. 1921? Lithograph, $17\,^1/_8 \times 20\,^3/_4''$. The Museum of Modern Art, New York

to mass printing, wood engraving became the chief means of illustration in newspapers, periodicals, and advertisements. The precision of nineteenth-century wood engraving offered a paradoxical contrast to the directness and simplicity of early woodcuts. But both lithography and wood engraving answered the growing need for the large quantities of cheaply printed pictures necessary for the instruction and amusement of modern man.

As the persistent demand for exact reproduction sacrificed original expression, the manufacture of prints became dominated by commercial printers and craftsmen, not by creative artists. Etching and engraving, already a century before, had been largely confined to the systematized reproduction of paintings and drawings.

The third graphic innovation of the nineteenth century not only revolutionized visual communication but completely surpassed the traditional print media as a means of creating multiple images. Photo-engraving, at last, offered a mechanical method of reproduction. It reduced to a minimum human interpretation and articulation. Slow, painstaking manual processes were no longer needed to make or reproduce pictures. Consequently a woodcut, an etching, a lithograph ceased to have social and economic importance as a means of communicating fact. At the same time printmaking, liberated from the bondage of reproduction, could again attract creative artists. Painters exreamined the graphic media: in etching, Manet, Degas, Whistler, and Ensor; in woodcut, Gauguin, Munch, and Vallotton; in lithography, the post-Impressionists in France.

In Germany the widespread revival of interest in printmaking waited until the end of the first decade of the twentieth century when, in Dresden, the first group of Expressionists returned to the woodcut, the medium with which the history of prints had begun. Four

Kollwitz: Plowmen. 1905. Etching with pencil corrections, $17\,^1/_2 \times 23''$. Collection Walter Bareiss, Greenwich, Connecticut

painters of an older generation, however, had been frequent etchers and lithographers.

Today Max Klinger's hallucinatory world of silent nightmare seems dated, but his technical facility as an engraver on metal astounded his contemporaries and certainly influenced the early work of Paul Klee. In Berlin after 1900 the Impressionist triumvirate, Max Liebermann, Max Slevogt, and Lovis Corinth, followed traditions begun in France. Liebermann's etchings of shimmering shade and light capture more successfully than his paintings the transitory effects he sought. Slevogt's best lithographs, the dramatic illustrations to James Fenimore Cooper's "The Leatherstocking Tales," were confined between the covers of a book. Corinth composed several series of etchings and lithographs, and, before his paintings, developed a loose but forceful style.

Two women, Paula Modersohn-Becker and Käthe Kollwitz, stand between post-Impressionism and the Expressionists. Modersohn-Becker's few etchings, like her paintings, reveal a highly personal and decorative adaptation of Gauguin. Kollwitz, almost entirely a graphic artist, passed from the influence of Klinger to a more expressive style. Illustrative, somewhat sentimental expositions on proletarian themes constitute her early work (page 187). Later, her protest and sympathy become less particularized and more direct.

Ernst Ludwig Kirchner's memory was vivid, if not exact. In 1937 he wrote to Curt Valentin: "Did you know that as far back as 1900 I had the audacious idea of revitalizing German art? Indeed I did and the impulse came to me while looking at an exhibition . . .

Schmidt-Rottluff: Erich Heckel. 1909. Lithograph, $15\,^5/_8 \times 12\,^5/_8''$.
The Museum of Modern Art, New York, James Thrall Soby Fund

Kirchner: Frau Dr. R. Binswanger. 1917.
Woodcut, $21\,^3/_4 \times 8\,^1/_2''$. The Museum
of Modern Art, New York

Inside hung these anemic, bloodless, lifeless studio daubs. Outside was life, noisy and colorful, pulsating ... First I tried to find a method whereby I could seize the effect of motion ... how to arrest, in a few bold strokes, a movement catching the passing moment and finding new forms ... My sense of design was simplified and strengthened by the fact that I had learned to make woodcuts from my father when I was only fifteen. So armed I arrived in Dresden and during my studies I was able to arouse my friends' enthusiasm for my new ideas."

Shortly after his twenty-first birthday in 1901, Kirchner completed his "gymnasium" courses at Chemnitz and entered the Technische Hochschule in Dresden as a student of architecture. Four years later Kirchner and three fellow students founded the first group of German Expressionists, Die Brücke (The Bridge). They were to constitute the first avant-garde reaction against a tradition already academic, the late realistic Impressionism of Liebermann, Slevogt, and Corinth.

Kirchner's friends were Fritz Bleyl, Erich Heckel, and Karl Schmidt-Rottluff. Kirchner had known Bleyl since 1902 and, under his instruction, carved linoleum cuts. In 1904 they met Heckel who, in turn, introduced them to Schmidt-Rottluff. After the summer, the younger Heckel and Schmidt-Rottluff dropped their studies and the four artists decided to form an association to further their economic livelihood. Schmidt-Rottluff contributed the name Künstlergruppe Brücke, and their first exhibition was held in a rented studio. A second group exhibition, somewhat more accessible to the public, was organized a year later in a Dresden lamp factory. From the outset printmaking was as important as painting in their program.

The Brücke manifesto, written by Kirchner and printed as a woodcut, read: "With a belief in the development of a new generation of creators and appreciators, we summon all youth. As those who will bear the burden of the future, we are determined to create for ourselves a physical and spiritual freedom opposed to established and traditional forces. He who portrays directly, without qualification, the creative impulse is one of us."

During 1906 three additional painters were invited to participate in the society's activities – Emil Nolde, their elder by some fifteen years; Max Pechstein, their contemporary; and the Swiss painter Cuno Amiet. Otto Mueller, from Berlin, joined in 1910.

The formation of the Brücke in Dresden coincides, in time, with the looser association of the Fauves in France. However, the early Brücke style – arbitrary patterns of color flatly arranged in broad, fluid designs (page 190) – was formulated later, not earlier than 1908, certainly under the influence of Matisse if not other members of the Fauves. Angular violence of design came even later, after the actual dissolution of the group, and was to be developed most by Kirchner, Heckel, Schmidt-Rottluff, and Pechstein (pages 193-194). From its inception Kirchner appeared as the dominant and most articulate personality of the Brücke, but the problem of dating his work between 1905 and

Kirchner: Girls on the Banks of the Elbe.
c. 1910. Color lithograph, $12^7/_8 \times 15''$.
Walter Bareiss, Greenwich, Connecticut

1915 needs thorough research. For instance, through Gustav Schiefler, the cataloguer of his prints, he assigned to the period 1898-1902 a woodcut dated in his own hand 1907; or, again, a woodcut known to be carved in 1922 was dated by Kirchner 1914 (cat. no. 79). Both prints are in the collection of the Museum of Modern Art in New York.

The Fauves and the Brücke were deeply influenced by the post-Impressionists, the Brücke, particularly by primitive art. Indeed it appears that the Brücke artists were making discoveries in the Dresden ethnographic museum well before the French artists began collecting Negro sculpture. Both groups exploited unnatural color and bold distortion. The neurotic melancholy, the brooding introspection so characteristic of the German Expressionists is alien to the Fauves, however, and reveals a greater debt to Munch than to van Gogh or Gauguin. The more intimate, daily association of the German artists gave the Brücke a cohesion as a brotherhood which the Fauves neither sought

190

Heckel: White Horses. 1912. Color woodcut,
$12^1/_8 \times 12^3/_8''$. The Museum of Modern Art,
New York

nor desired. Until 1911 the members worked in close collaboration, sharing living and working quarters in Dresden and vacationing together during the summers. They freely exchanged cover designs for portfolios of each other's prints and often used the same stones for their lithographs.

Berlin, the capital, provided better opportunities for sale and exhibition than did Dresden. For instance in 1910 a large exhibition in Berlin devoted to prints featured each member of the Brücke. Berlin was also the permanent residence of Otto Mueller, and between 1910 and 1911 he was joined by Pechstein, Kirchner, Heckel, and Schmidt-Rottluff.

Nolde had remained affiliated with the society only a year and a half. Fritz Bleyl had resigned as an active member in 1909 to devote himself to teaching. The move to Berlin spelled the final disintegration of the group Success, or desire for success, as individuals rather than as members of a brotherhood accelerated the breakup. Kirchner's volatile and domineering personality to no small extent contributed. The artists had agreed to exhibit only jointly. Pechstein, the first to receive a measure of recognition, broke the rule and was expelled. There was dissension and recrimination. Kirchner's "Chronicle of the Brücke" of 1913, again composed as a woodcut, attempted to speak for the remaining members. The manifesto, fatal as well as final, was rejected by both Heckel and Schmidt-Rottluff. Only the gentle Mueller remained faithful to Kirchner, and his work is least typical of the group.

The Brücke had worked in the three basic print processes: woodcut, lithography, and intaglio. Prints not only increased the variety of media for expression but, since they are multiple, helped propagandize the new group. The public, invited to join as active or lay members, was solicited with subscription prints. Manifestos, posters, stationery, announcements, annual reports, membership cards all consisted of woodcuts and lithographs. In addition, between 1906 and 1911, the society published six portfolios devoted to the work of single or of several members.

"There is no way to study an artist better than by his graphic work," wrote Kirchner, and "the woodcut is the most graphic of the print processes." The first Brücke prints were woodcuts and in them reappears a tradition that seems essentially Germanic —

Kirchner: Street Crossing, Leipzig. 1915-16. Lithograph, $23\,^1/_2 \times 20''$. Collection Walter Bareiss, Connecticut

Kirchner: Otto Mueller. 1915. Color woodcut, $10^7/_8 \times 21^1/_2''$. Collection Dr. Bernhard Sprengel, Hanover

the boldness and crudeness of Gothic prints, the intensity of Baldung's woodcuts and Grünewald's drawing, a direct appeal to the emotions. The Brücke's actual method of carving wood, however, followed a more recent tradition established by Gauguin and the Norwegian Edvard Munch, a resident of Germany until 1908. Through the distribution of his prints Munch, more than any other single artist, is the father of Expressionism.

The woodcut had provided Gauguin with a medium particularly suited to the primitive attitude he wished to assume. He exposed the texture of the material itself by leaving areas of the surface uncut, flat, to contrast the boldness of his carving with the roughness of the wood. Gauguin's innovations, an abrupt break with the meticulous, reproductive craftsmanship of the nineteenth-century wood-engravers, became the foundation of the modern woodcut. Munch used larger blocks, and the stylization of his forms, often highly abstract, evolved from the way in which the wood could be most effectively worked. Félix Vallotton, the Swiss artist associated with Bonnard and Vuillard in France, was the third master of the woodcut to influence the group. Unlike Munch and Gauguin he did not work in color, but his decorative massing of black against white set an example for many Brücke prints.

Schmidt-Rottluff: The Miraculous Draught of Fishes. 1918. Woodcut, 15$^{1}/_{2}$ × 19$^{5}/_{8}$". Collection Mrs. Gertrud A. Mellon, New York

In 1907 Schmidt-Rottluff introduced lithography, which he had just learned, to the other members of the society. From the outset they disdained transfer paper (so often used in France) and drew directly on the stone. The insistent appearance of the actual edge of the stone in Kirchner's and Nolde's lithographs is characteristic of the Brücke as printmakers. Lithography also invites the freedom of the brush, and many of their lithographs seem more spontaneous and less schematized than their woodcuts.

As works of art the prints of the Brücke artists are frequently more convincing than their paintings. Many of their best prints repeat the subjects of their paintings and, in the translation and reduction to a graphic medium, gain a maximum of effect by a minimum of means. Kirchner himself tried to explain "the mysterious attraction" of prints. "Perhaps the urge which drives the artist to printmaking is partly due to the effort to fix in final form what in drawing remains loose and unpredictable. The actual technical manipulations release in the artist powers which do not come into play in the much easier handiwork of drawing and painting. The process of printing welds the previous and separate steps into a unity."

Heckel: Nude (Fränzi). 1911. Color woodcut, $14^7/_8 \times 10^7/_8''$.
Collection Walter Bareiss, Greenwich, Connecticut

Nolde: Scribes. 1911. Etching and aquatint, $10\,^1/_2 \times 11\,^3/_4''$. The Museum of Modern Art, New York

Ernst Ludwig Kirchner produced more than 1700 woodcuts, lithographs, and etchings, in quantity a graphic oeuvre unequalled by any modern artist. His need for expression as a printmaker was compulsive, and, without any reference to his painting, his character and quality as an artist can be determined through his graphic work.

The realistic naturalism of his early style disappeared under the influence of the Jugendstil and Vallotton. By 1908, under the impact of Munch, the formal and psychological strength of his own prints pointed the direction he was to follow. The subsequent broader and looser drawing of his Brücke lithographs between 1909 and 1911 acknowledged the Fauves (page 190); but the next years saw bolder distortion and a more dramatic balance between strident color and simplified form (page 193).

The direct, slashing strokes and sharp edges of Kirchner's paintings derive as much

Nolde: Grotesques. 1913. Color lithograph, $23^1/_4 \times 19''$. The Museum of Modern Art, New York

Nolde: Young Couple. 1913. Color lithograph, $24^1/_2 \times 20''$. The Museum of Modern Art, New York

from his woodcut techniques as from the intensity of his emotions. The strongest tensions in his art, however, appear most clearly in black and white, for instance the portrait of Frau Binswanger where lines of white instead of black delineate the forms (page 189). His color woodcuts are, of course, more painterly in their effect; and, to add color to many of his lithographs in black, he printed on a lemon-colored paper. The flat patterns and the angular violence of his designs are perhaps most successful when he transfixes passing moments of everyday reality into arresting stylizations of movement.

During the 1920s the force of his prints as well as his paintings surrenders to a style less harsh and more relaxed. The increasing curvilinear treatment of form recalls the Jugendstil of his youth as well as certain contemporary works by Picasso. They perilously approach decorative abstraction.

Erich Heckel made about 900 prints, perhaps a third of which are woodcuts. His best graphic work, unlike that of Kirchner, belongs specifically to the Brücke period. The psychological obsessions of Kirchner did not disturb Heckel and, if his woodcuts seem less bold, they are nevertheless reflective, sensitive, and graced by humor – the amusing stance of Fränzi (page 195), the expectant moment before a storm (page 191), and, later, the quiet introspection of his own self portrait. Like Kirchner, Heckel often allowed the shape of the block to determine the over-all limits of the composition.

In an effort to discover the vitality of the primitive, Karl Schmidt-Rottluff achieved only the mannerism of the archaic. The style of his painting, more convincing than his emotion, evolved from his experience as a carver of woodcuts. It was about Schmidt-Rottluff's prints, robust if heavy, that Munch exclaimed: "May God preserve us, there will be difficult times ahead!"

Schmidt-Rottluff produced more than 300 woodcuts, only one or two in color, as well as lithographs and a few etchings. In comparison with his early work (page 188), the schematization of his forms appears arbitrary and routine. Though his striking black-and-white idiom was formed by 1912, his most memorable prints are perhaps those

Nolde: The Doctors. 1922. Woodcut, $19^7/_8$ $\times 27^3/_4$". The Museum of Modern Art, gift of Mrs. John D. Rockefeller, Jr.

left, Nolde: Windmill on the Shore. 1929. Color lithograph, $24\,^5/_8 \times 32\,^1/_2''$. The Museum of Modern Art, New York, James Thrall Soby Fund.
right, Mueller: Two Gypsies. 1927. Color lithograph, $27\,^1/_2 \times 19\,^1/_2''$. Collection Walter Bareiss, Greenwich, Connecticut

of 1917-1919 based on religious themes (page 194). These recall Gothic woodcuts, but their style seems more heathen than Christian. Indeed the heads of Christ and His disciples are unabashedly derived from African masks.

Otto Mueller carved few woodcuts. Perhaps the directness of the medium could not enhance the romantic, if monotonous, arcadia of his pastorals. Mild, always felicitous, his work is not sparked by the vitality of the other Brücke members. He himself acknowledged as his most distinguished graphic achievement the suite of color lithographs on gypsy themes composed in 1927 (above).

When Emil Nolde joined the group in Dresden in 1906, he was already an accomplished and highly original etcher. He remained affiliated with the Brücke only a year and a half; the association, although brief, was important. He instructed the other members in the chemistry of etching. In intaglio, however, the work of Kirchner and Heckel seems tentative, even scratchy. Nolde's etchings surpass those of the other members and, more than his paintings, they reveal the influence of that other fantasist, James Ensor, whom he met in 1912 (page 196).

Marc: Tigers. 1912. Woodcut, $7\,^7/_8 \times 9\,^1/_2''$.
The Museum of Modern Art, New York

From the Brücke Nolde learned woodcut and lithography. The example of the younger artists also stimulated the development of his own personal style. He returned to Schleswig in northern Germany, and in 1913 in a printer's workshop, became fascinated by the possibilities of lithography. Over and over again he pulled the same composition in an almost endless series of variations in color. The Young Couple (page 197) is only one of some 72 different printings from the same stones.

Nolde's graphic oeuvre numbers some 500 etchings, lithographs and woodcuts. Unlike the Brücke artists, he did not ordinarily repeat the subjects of his paintings but instead expanded the themes of his art. The wild gestures of his figures and the shaggy contours of his drawing offer a peculiar combination of the Gothic, the grotesque, the lyric, and the deeply religious. His description of the artist is ecstatic: "The devil dwells in his limbs, divinity in his heart. Who can realize these powers fighting with one another in endless conflict? Behind walls lives the artist, rarely in flight, often in his snail's shell. He loves the rarest and most profound natural occurrences, but also the bright, the ordinary reality, moving clouds and blooming, growing flowers, the living creatures. Unknown, unknowing creatures are his friends. He sees not much, but other men see nothing."

In Dresden the organization of the Brücke had lasted from 1905 until 1911. The second group of Expressionists, the Blaue Reiter, proclaimed itself in Munich in 1911. Franz Marc and Kandinsky were joined by several other painters, among them Macke, Heinrich Campendonk, Jawlensky, and Klee. They formed a more cosmopolitan association than the Brücke; Kandinsky and Jawlensky were Russian, Klee had been born in Switzerland. They freely acknowledged the school of Paris and particularly admired Cézanne, Rousseau, Picasso, and Delaunay. Unlike the Brücke, their interest in ethnographic art was slight; instead they found inspiration in the folk arts of Germany and the Near East.

The Blaue Reiter lacked the stylistic cohesion of the Brücke. The attitude of the individual members was extremely varied but, banded together to form an active program of exhibition, they aroused far more controversy. It is difficult to establish their real identity as a group; but the lyric idealizations of Marc are, in spirit, not too removed from the revelations of Kandinsky's early abstractions.

The Blaue Reiter did not consider printmaking as important as painting, and the woodcuts of Marc, Macke, and Campendonk lack the scale and force of those of the Brücke. The boldest conceptions were the animal fantasies of Marc (opposite); Campendonk's more rustic, bucolic world owes much to Chagall. Macke's few woodcuts present a similar idyllic life although they describe neither peasant manners nor domesticated beasts. In their deliberate naïveté the prints of all three artists were influenced by the first woodcuts of Kandinsky, little-known illustrations to fairy tales and folk legends.

Kandinsky and Klee used lithography, etching, and, very occasionally, woodcut. The

Marcks: Bat. 1948. Woodcut, 8 5/8 × 9″. The Museum of Modern Art, New York, gift of Mrs. Donald B. Straus

left, Kokoschka: Man and Woman with Candle. 1913. Lithograph, $13^1/_8 \times 10^1/_2''$. The Museum of Modern Art, New York. *right,* Kokoschka: Wanderer. 1914. Lithograph, $16^3/_8 \times 12^3/_8''$. The Museum of Modern Art, New York

careers of both artists, however, transcend identification with any particular group. Of all the Blaue Reiter, Klee was the most versatile printmaker. Jawlensky's few lithographs are feeble; Kandinsky's most characteristic prints were produced after 1920.

Three Expressionists, Kokoschka, Beckmann, and Rohlfs, were prolific graphic artists. When Kokoschka arrived in Berlin in 1910 he had already formulated his personal style. Like many Expressionists he planned most of his prints in cycles around specific themes. Essentially a painter, it is only natural that he confined himself to lithography. The illustrations to his own play "Der Gefesselte Columbus" (above left) describe a basic antagonism between the sexes, as in Munch, the chief inspiration of his early work. The later lithographs to a Bach cantata portray the same elemental conflict in a less obsessive fashion. Kokoschka's striking self portrait (opposite), one of the most pene-

Kokoschka: Self Portrait. 1923. Color lithograph, $24^1/_2 \times 18^3/_8''$. The Museum of Modern Art, New York

left, Rohlfs: Prisoner. 1918. Woodcut, $24^1/_8 \times 18^1/_8''$. The Museum of Modern Art, New York. *right,* Rohlfs: Return of the Prodigal Son. 1916. Woodcut, $19^3/_4 \times 14^3/_8''$. The Museum of Modern Art, New York

trating Expressionist analyses, completely overshadows his more recent attempts at color lithography. Unfortunately in his prints he has ignored landscape and the sweeping panoramic vistas so characteristic of his painting.

In Berlin Max Beckmann's early work (page 206), mature and complete in itself, was allied to the realism of Slevogt and Corinth. The first World War accelerated a break with this tradition, and the suffering and carnage served as a terrible inspiration. Beckmann himself was hospitalized in 1915, and for a brief time ceased painting to begin printmaking. In Frankfurt until 1933, he continued to make many drypoints, an intaglio method of scratching metal which requires few tools or equipment. The crowded images of his early drypoints, often grotesque in their combination of horror and humor, culminated in the series of lithographs entitled "Hell." From this portfolio is The Night (page 214), a repetition of a painting. The turbulent composition, the sadistic executioners, the garroted man, and broken woman create a bedlam as gruesome as it was pro-

204

left, Barlach: The Good Samaritan. 1919. Woodcut, $7 \times 5''$. *right,* Barlach: Group in a Storm. 1919. Woodcut, $7 \times 5''$. The Museum of Modern Art, New York, given anonymously

phetic. Almost serene in comparison are the café scene (page 207) and his large-scale woodcuts. Their objectivity and lack of ferocity reflect a natural reaction against the violence of his previous work. Except for the series of lithographs, "Day and Dream" (1946), Beckmann made few prints in his last years.

Christian Rohlfs, the oldest of the Expressionists, was born a century ago. Unlike Kokoschka and Beckmann who elude classification with any specific group, Rohlfs in his woodcuts suggests a close affinity with the Brücke and therefore Munch. Rohlfs made many prints, 155 woodcuts, 22 linoleum cuts, and a pair of lithographs. His work is positive, and even The Prisoner (opposite), his most memorable graphic image, lacks the self-inflicted guilt and torment of Kokoschka and Beckmann.

The sculptors of twentieth-century Germany have usually composed prints. The graphic work of Lehmbruck, Kolbe, and Sintenis, however, is completely incidental. Lehmbruck's etchings too often expose a perverse eroticism that seems alien to the nobility of his sculptured figures. His prints are minor, even sketchy, and the illustration for "Macbeth" (opposite) is not typical. Kolbe's expressive nudes and the charming bestiary of Sintenis reappear in their etchings. None of the three artists attempted wood carving in either sculpture or prints.

In all his work Ernst Barlach's style remained consistent – earthy, robust, often passionate, deceptively simple. Although decorative, his distortions are never arbitrary. His works speak with the eloquence of the medieval sculptures and Gothic woodcuts which inspired him. A distinguished contributor to the German theatre, Barlach illustrated his own four plays and composed prints on Christian themes. Even when his work is not specifically religious, Barlach, like Nolde, is moved by a deeply genuine faith. Unlike Kokoschka or Beckmann, he was convinced of the essential goodness of man. His illustrations broadened his subject matter, and lithography encouraged a rhythmic looseness in his draughtsmanship. Barlach's woodcuts on peasant themes, however, are more characteristic and repeat the directness of his sculptures (page 205).

Gerhard Marcks and Ewald Mataré have been prolific carvers of woodcuts. In their

Beckmann: David and Bathsheba. 1911. Lithograph, $12^3/_8 \times 9^3/_4''$.
The Museum of Modern Art, New York, James Thrall Soby Fund

left, Beckmann: Kasbek. 1923. Drypoint, $19^1/_2 \times 8^3/_8''$. The Museum of Modern Art, New York, gift of Victor S. Riesenfeld. *right,* Lehmbruck: Macbeth. 1918. Etching and drypoint, $15^1/_2 \times 11^3/_4''$. The Museum of Modern Art, Mrs. John D. Rockefeller, Jr. Fund

prints, as in their sculptures, the Expressionist tradition becomes less aggressive. Marcks, like Barlach, works in sharp contrasts of solid black and white; Mataré, like the Brücke artists, works in color and uses the grain of the wood for decorative effect. In recent years Marcks has illustrated several books, but his most striking woodcuts depict animal life (page 201) – the inspiration of Marc and the peaceable kingdom of Mataré.

Although Dada was the first modern movement to become truly international in its membership, the majority of its founders were German. In retrospect it might be considered another manifestation of the Expressionist spirit; but where the Brücke and the Blaue Reiter had revolted against realism, Dada denied reason itself.

Dada was born during the war in neutral Zurich. After the armistice it mushroomed

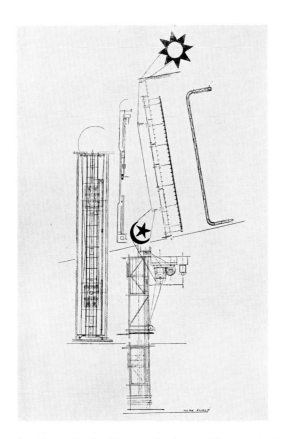
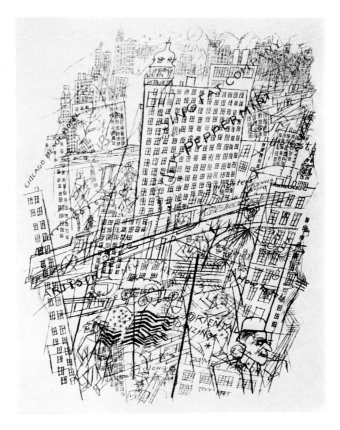

left, Ernst: Trophy, Hypertrophied. 1919. Photo-mechanical technical engraving altered with pen and ink, $13^{7}/_{8} \times 7^{1}/_{8}''$. The Museum of Modern Art, New York, gift of Tristan Tzara. *right*, Grosz: Memories of New York. 1917. Lithograph, $14^{3}/_{4} \times 11^{5}/_{8}''$. The Museum of Modern Art, New York

in Cologne, Berlin, and Hanover. Capricious and chaotic, destructive and always eager to shock, Dada's ridicule of bourgeois standards, like the monetary inflation, was symptomatic of Germany's bewildering unrest. Dada lacked any constructive objective. It served as a purgative. Like Surrealism, its successor, Dada was conceived as a literary as well as an artistic movement but, as writers assumed control, the spontaneity of the visual image surrendered to the dogma of the written word. Dada, as a manifestation, died in 1922. In the despair of post-war Germany, Berlin and Cologne Dada as opposed to New York or Paris Dada, had developed definite political doctrines, pacifist, often anarchist or communist. Its sentimental appeal to the proletariat, however, was unsuccessful.

Characteristically, Dada techniques in printmaking were neither orthodox nor conventional; the artists saw no reason not to use photography or mechanical aids. Today, a glance at the advertising layouts of any newspaper or periodical demonstrates the importance of their experiments in typography which in turn had been inspired by Italian Futurism.

In Cologne Max Ernst found blocks for technical engravings, reassembled them, and pulled prints which he gently altered with pen and ink. His Trophy, Hypertrophied (opposite), an hilarious piece of science fiction, was refused exhibition in Paris by the Section d'Or because it was not, strictly speaking, an original. Some of Hans Arp's earliest work had been etchings, but his "Arpaden," published in Hanover by Kurt Schwitters, were photo-mechanical renditions of drawings. Schwitters' own "Merz" portfolio also consists of photo-lithographs, mechanical reproductions of arrangements of cut-out papers and type, sometimes embellished with actual collage (page 210). In Berlin many of George Grosz' lithographs reproduced pen and ink drawings of different size.

Ernst's first album of prints, "Fiat Modes," owes much to the dream-world constructions of de Chirico. It anticipates Surrealism which, with André Breton, he was to launch in Paris in 1924. Grosz' lithograph, Memories of New York (opposite), offers a more typical Dada interest in sound and movement. His use of photomontage in the projected but unpublished "Dadaco" influenced the lithographs of Schwitters. Grosz, however, was dedicated to caricature and social protest. Schwitters, for his part, took little interest in political controversy.

Separately, but with Arp, Schwitters gave Dada discipline. His Merz went beyond the self-conscious madness of Dada. From mockery could grow the sobriety of abstraction. The calculated scale and sensitive balance of Schwitters' lithographs are not unrelated to the architectonic compositions of the Russian Lissitzky, also a resident of Hanover, who published two portfolios of lithographs, "Figurinen" (1921) and "Proun" (1923).

In 1919 the Bauhaus opened in Weimar. The first proclamation, written by the architect

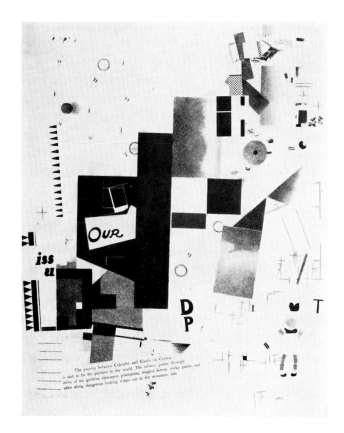 

left, Schwitters: Merz Composition. 1923. Process lithograph with collage, 21 $^1/_4$ × 17 $^1/_2$″. The Museum of Modern Art, New York, gift of J. B. Neumann. *right*, Klee: Destruction and Hope. 1916. Lithograph and watercolor, 18 $^3/_8$ × 13″. The Museum of Modern Art, New York

Walter Gropius, was ornamented with a woodcut by Lyonel Feininger. From its inception painters and sculptors were leading members of the faculty, and the student community included several artists who were permitted to devote themselves to painting. But the emphasis and impact of the Bauhaus was strongest upon architecture and applied design.

In printmaking the Bauhaus' most important contribution was its early, active program of publications. Between 1921 and 1923 portfolios of prints by Feininger (who had exhibited with the Blaue Reiter in 1913) and by Kandinsky and Marcks were printed and published at the school. In addition, the Bauhaus issued five albums of prints which included contributions from the faculty and miscellaneous artists. Interests in creative printmaking declined after the removal from Weimar to Dessau in 1925. Marcks had quit the faculty and, although Feininger continued instruction in etching and woodcut, the courses increasingly stressed typography and layout.

Before their association with the Bauhaus, Klee and Feininger had produced many prints. Marcks' interest in woodcut, however, seems to have begun in Weimar. The identifying stamp of the Bauhaus as a school, the unity between architecture and painting, is found more characteristically in the work of other members. The prints of Schlemmer, Moholy-Nagy and, later, Vordemberge-Gildewart, typical of their individual styles, are few and incidental. Kandinsky, at the Bauhaus, lost the free expressiveness of his early abstractions. Only a few plates of his "Kleine Welten," a portfolio of four etchings, four lithographs and four woodcuts of 1922, come to life. As decorative geometry, a larger composition of the next year is more effective (below).

Feininger's first prints, lithographs and etchings (1906-1912), evoke a nostalgia for the ships and trains which had captured his imagination as a child in America. In 1918 he began to carve his first woodcuts and, during the next dozen years, continued wood-

Kandinsky: Abstraction. 1923. Color lithograph,
16 × 15 1/8". The Museum of Modern Art, New York

cut and painting as parallel means of expression. Since he was an instructor in the graphic arts, it is not unnatural that his years at the Bauhaus were his most productive as a printmaker. Many of his woodcuts repeat themes of early paintings and prints. Their disjointed rhythm and angular distortion, however, depart from the narrative romanticism of his previous work and seem admirably suited to the medium of the woodcut. Architecture is forcibly integrated into a nervous pattern of black and white in the Buildings (page 184), while his most famous print, The Gate, stands as a more monumental combination of strength and decoration. Feininger made more than a hundred prints, two-thirds of which are woodcuts. In both his prints and paintings, he refrained from the schematized abstractions so often characteristic of the Bauhaus.

The prints of Paul Klee number about 110, divided almost equally between etching and lithography. In Switzerland he completed fourteen etchings (1903-1905), perverse in their realism and precise in their style. These sophisticated parables, "inventions" he called them, were conceived with elaborate captions written into the metal plates. Klee considered the series his first independent achievement as an artist.

In Germany, between 1910 and 1932, Klee continued to make a few prints each year. He began lithography in 1912 and continued to work on stone or transfer paper until 1927. Several of these lithographs were printed in color, or colored by hand. When Klee left Germany to return to Switzerland he ceased printmaking.

In terms of his development as an artist Klee's later prints, important though they are, do not have the significance of the early suite of etchings. They are however much more than echoes of his paintings and drawings. The complex of Little World is a forerunner of Dada cityscapes; Destruction and Hope (page 210) approaches abstraction. More familiar are the lackadaisical, Steamer for Lugano (opposite), the intense The One in Love, and the elliptical calligraphy of Why Does He Run? (opposite).

In Germany the phrase Neue Sachlichkeit (new realism or new objectivity) was invented to describe the inevitable reaction against Expressionism and abstraction. Otto Dix and George Grosz had both worked in a Dada idiom, bitter and satiric. But their most typical work, in their prints as in their paintings, was done after 1921. Dix's sustained group of etchings "Der Krieg" (page 215) invite deliberate comparison with Goya's indictment of war. Their realism is horrible, unflinching and overwhelming; the portfolio could appropriately have been reissued after the second war. Less profound are his single prints, although the Mediterranean Sailor bristles with a humor coarse and sharp.

Grosz' draughtsmanship is more mordant, his criticism scathing. After a few early etchings he confined himself to lithography, and most of his prints were composed in series. His derisive attacks bite the bourgeois and the military. The Dada effects of noise in Christmas Eve (page 215) add no charm of genre to the family gathering.

Klee: Why Does He Run? 1932. Etching, $9\,^3/_8 \times$
$11\,^3/_4''$. The Museum of Modern Art, New York

Klee: Steamer for Lugano. 1922. Lithograph,
$10\,^7/_8 \times 15\,^3/_8''$. Private collection, New York

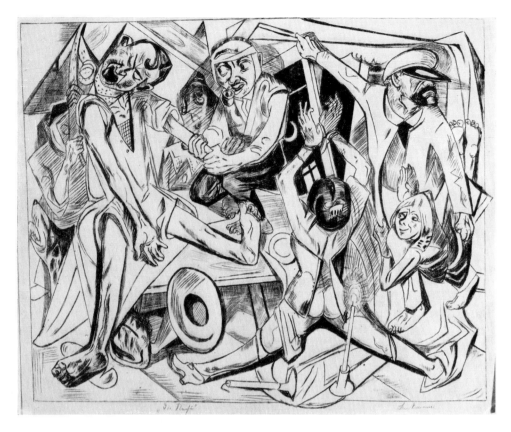

Beckmann: The Night. 1919. Lithograph, $21\,^7/_8 \times 27\,^5/_8''$. The Museum of Modern Art, New York

The "new realism" could not supplant Expressionism or abstraction. It did attract, however, several other artists – Beckmann, briefly; George Scholz whose lithographs are unmitigated in their bitter humor; and, more mildly, Georg Schrimpf and Alexander Kanoldt.

From the United States it is of course difficult to evaluate German printmaking in recent years. Artists such as Marcks and Mataré have continued to produce many woodcuts, but in general creative printmaking declined during the Third Reich. The reputation of three artists, however, has been established since the war. Rolf Nesch now lives in Norway, but his highly developed and personal techniques of intaglio were formulated in Germany by 1932 (page 217). Helmut Grieshaber lives in isolation on the mountain of Achalin in Würtemberg, but the bold, decorative patterns of his color woodcuts (page 216) continue the tradition of the Brücke. Hans Hartung has been a

Grosz: Christmas Eve. 1921. Lithograph, $18\,^1/_4 \times 14\,^1/_4''$.
The Museum of Modern Art, New York, gift of Paul J. Sachs

Dix: Wounded, Fall 1916, Bapaume. 1924. Etching and aquatint, $7\,^3/_4 \times 11\,^3/_8''$. The Museum
of Modern Art, New York, gift of Mrs. John D. Rockefeller, Jr.

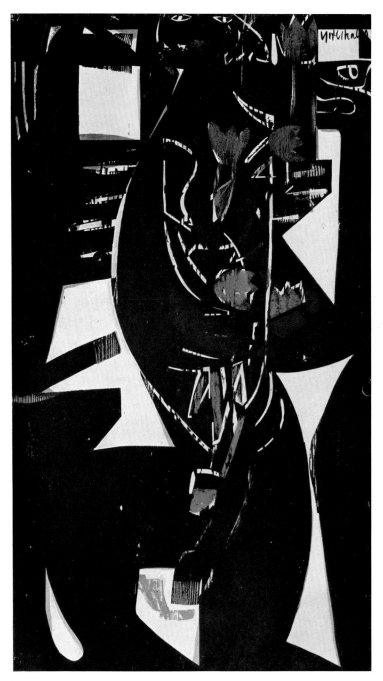

Grieshaber: Elysium. 1953. Color woodcut, $43\,^1/_2 \times 24\,^1/_4''$. The Museum of
Modern Art. New York, gift of Mr. and Mrs. E. Powis Jones

Nesch : Free Port Bridge, Hamburg. 1932. Aquatint, $17\,^3/_4 \times 23\,^1/_2''$. The Museum of Modern Art, New York

resident of France for two decades. His etchings in color, like his paintings, belong to the School of Paris.

The selection of prints included in the present exhibition has been determined by those artists already represented by painting and sculpture. Ideally, any summary of modern German prints should begin with Slevogt and Liebermann. Pechstein would be included with the Brücke, Campendonk with the Blaue Reiter and, among many other possible inclusions, Arp, Moholy-Nagy, Vordemberge-Gildewart, Scholz, and Kanoldt. In addition to Jawlensky and Kandinsky, work produced by other Russian artists resident in Germany, Chagall, Archipenko, and Lissitzky, might also have been added. Kollwitz, Nesch, and Grieshaber are the only artists in the exhibition not also represented by paintings or sculpture. Their work is almost exclusively confined to the graphic arts.

WILLIAM S. LIEBERMAN

catalogue of the exhibition

The Museum of Modern Art, New York: October 1-December 8,1957
City Art Museum of St. Louis: January 8-February 24, 1958

In dimensions height precedes width

BARLACH, Ernst   1870-1938

1   *Man in Stocks.* 1918. Wood, 28$^3/_4$″ high. Kunsthalle, Hamburg. Ill. p.149

2   *The Good Samaritan.* 1919. Woodcut, 7 × 5″. The Museum of Modern Art, New York, given anonymously. Ill. p. 205

3   *Group in a Storm.* 1919. Woodcut, 7 × 5″. The Museum of Modern Art, New York, given anonymously. Ill. p.205

4a *The Avenger.* 1922. Wood, 24″ high. Herman Schulman Collection, New York. (Exhibited in New York only). Ill. p.151

 b *The Avenger.* 1922. Bronze (cast 1923), 24″ high. Fine Arts Associates, New York. (Exhibited in St. Louis only)

5   *Singing Man.* 1928. Bronze, 19$^1/_2$″ high. The Museum of Modern Art, New York, Mrs. John D. Rockefeller, Jr. Fund. Ill. p.152

BAUM, Otto   born 1900

6   *Metamorphosis.* 1948-49. Limestone, 39$^3/_8$″ high. Owned by the artist. Ill. p.176

BAUMEISTER, Willi   1889-1955

7   *Composition.* c. 1925? Color lithograph, 15$^3/_4$ × 9$^1/_8$″. The Museum of Modern Art, New York, Purchase 1936

8   *Homage to Jerome Bosch.* 1953. Oil on composition board, 43$^1/_4$ × 59″. Collection Mrs. Margarete Baumeister, Stuttgart. Color plate p.131

9   *Montaru I.* 1953. Oil on cardboard, 39$^5/_8$ × 51$^1/_4$″. Niedersächsische Landesgalerie, Hanover. Ill. p.132

BECKMANN, Max   1884-1950

10 *David and Bathsheba.* 1911. Lithograph, 12$^3/_8$ × 9$^3/_4$″. The Museum of Modern Art, New York, James Thrall Soby Fund. Ill. p. 206

11 *The Night.* 1919. Lithograph, 21$^7/_8$ × 27$^5/_8$″ From "Die Hölle," a portfolio of 10 lithographs, published by J.B. Neumann, Berlin. The Museum of Modern Art, New York, Purchase 1949. Ill. p.214

12 *Family Picture.* 1920. Oil on canvas, 25$^5/_8$ × 39$^3/_4$″. The Museum of Modern Art, New York, gift of Mrs. John D. Rockefeller, Jr. Ill. p. 100

13 *Kasbek.* 1923. Drypoint, 19$^1/_2$ × 8$^3/_8$″. The Museum of Modern Art, gift of Victor S. Riesenfeld. Ill. p. 207

14 *Café Concert in the Hotel.* 1924. Woodcut, 19$^1/_2$ × 19$^5/_8$″. The Museum of Modern Art, New York, Purchase 1948

15 *View of Genoa.* 1927. Oil on canvas, 35$^1/_2$ × 66$^1/_2$″. Collection Mr. and Mrs. Morton D. May, St. Louis. Color plate p. 101

16 *Rugby Players.* 1929. Oil on canvas, 84$^7/_8$ × 39$^3/_8$″. Städtisches Museum, Duisburg. Color plate p. 102

17 *The Bath.* 1931. Oil on canvas, 70 × 48″. Collection Mr. and Mrs. Morton D. May, St. Louis, Missouri. Color plate p. 103

18 *Temptation.* 1936. Oil on canvas; triptych, center panel 79 × 67″, side panels each 84$^3/_4$ × 39$^1/_4$″. Collection Dr. Stephan Lackner, Santa Barbara, California. Color plate pp. 104-105

BELLING, Rudolf   born 1886

19 *Sculpture.* 1923. Bronze, partly silvered, 18$^7/_8$″ high. The Museum of Modern Art, New York, A. Conger Goodyear Fund. Ill. p. 174

BLUMENTHAL, Hermann   1905-1942

20 *Kneeling Youth.* 1929-30. Bronze (cast 1947), 40$^1/_2$″ high. Ehemals Staatliche Museen Berlin, National Gallery, on loan from the Kulturkreis im Bundesverband der deutschen Industrie. Ill. p. 179

CORINTH, Lovis   1858—1925

21 *Studio Corner.* 1919. Drypoint, 12$^3/_8$ × 9″. From "Bei den Corinthern," a portfolio of 14 etchings and drypoints. The Museum of Modern Art, New York, given anonymously

22 *Death and the Artist.* 1921. Etching and drypoint, $9^3/_8 \times 7''$. From "Totentanz," a series of 5 etchings published by Euphorion-Verlag, Berlin, 1922. The Museum of Modern Art, New York, gift of J. B. Neumann

23 *Apocalypse.* c.1921? Lithograph, $17^1/_8 \times 20^3/_4''$. The Museum of Modern Art, New York, given anonymously. Ill. p.186

24 *Near the Walchensee – Silver Way.* 1923. Oil on canvas, $23^1/_4 \times 35''$. Collection Mr. and Mrs. Erich Cohn, New York. Ill. p.73

25 *Self Portrait.* 1924. Oil on canvas, $39^3/_8 \times 31^5/_8''$. The Museum of Modern Art, New York, gift of Curt Valentin. Color plate p.72

26 *Winter at Walchensee.* 1924. Watercolor, $16 \times 18^1/_4''$. Collection Mr. and Mrs. Erich Cohn, New York. Ill. p.73

DIX, Otto   born 1891

27 *Mediterranean Sailor.* 1923. Lithograph, $18 \times 12^1/_2''$. The Museum of Modern Art, New York, Purchase 1945

28 *My Parents.* 1924. Oil on canvas, $45^7/_8 \times 51^1/_4''$. Nieder-sächsische Landesgalerie, Hanover. Color plate p.86

29 *Wounded, Fall 1916, Bapaume.* 1924. Etching and aquatint, $7^3/_4 \times 11^3/_8''$. From "Der Krieg," a portfolio of 50 etchings, published by Karl Nierendorf, Berlin. The Museum of Modern Art, New York, gift of Mrs. John D. Rockefeller Jr. Ill. p.215

30 *Dr. Mayer-Hermann.* 1926. Oil on wood, $58^3/_4 \times 39''$. The Museum of Modern Art, New York, gift of Philip C. Johnson. (Exhibited in New York only). Ill. p.88

31 *Child with Doll.* 1928. Oil on wood, $29^1/_4 \times 15^1/_4''$. The Museum of Modern Art, New York, gift of Mrs. John D. Rockefeller, Jr. (Exhibited in St. Louis only). Ill. p.89

ERNST, Max   born 1891

32 *Trophy, Hypertrophied.* 1919. Photo-mechanical technical engraving altered with pen and ink, $13^7/_8 \times 7^1/_8''$. The Museum of Modern Art, New York, gift of Tristan Tzara. Ill. p.208

33 *"Let there be fashion, down with art."* c.1919. Lithograph, $16^1/_8 \times 11^1/_2''$. From "Fiat modes, pereat ars," a portfolio of 8 lithographs, published by Schlömilch Verlag, Cologne. The Museum of Modern Art, New York, Purchase 1935

34 *The Hat Makes the Man (bedecktsamiger stapel-mensch nacktsamiger wasserformer ["edelformer"] kleidsame nervatur. auch! umpressnerven!).* 1920. Collage, pencil, ink, watercolor, $14 \times 18''$. The Museum of Modern Art, New York, Purchase 1935. Ill. p.90

35 *The Little Tear Gland That Says Tic Tac.* 1920. Gouache on wallpaper, $14^1/_4 \times 10''$. The Museum of Modern Art, New York, Purchase 1935. Ill. p.92

36 *The Gramineous Bicycle Garnished with Bells the Dappled Fire Damps and the Echinoderms Bending the Spine to Look for Caresses.* 1920 or 1921. Anatomical chart altered with gouache, $29^1/_4 \times 39^1/_4''$. The Museum of Modern Art, New York, Purchase 1937. Ill. p.91

FEININGER, Lyonel   1871-1956

37 *The Side Wheeler.* 1913. Oil on canvas, $31^3/_4 \times 39^5/_8''$. The Detroit Institute of Arts, Detroit, Michigan. Ill. p.107

38 *Bridge III.* 1917. Oil on canvas, $31^1/_2 \times 39^3/_8''$. Wallraf-Richartz Museum, Cologne. Color plate p.109

39 *Buildings.* 1919. Woodcut, $18^1/_2 \times 14^3/_8''$. The Museum of Modern Art, New York, gift of Mrs. Lyonel Feininger. Ill. p.184

40 *The Gate.* 1920. Woodcut, $16 \times 17^3/_4''$. The Museum of Modern Art, New York, James Thrall Soby Fund

41 *Barfüsser-Church in Erfurt (Barfüsser-Kirche in Erfurt).* 1927. Oil on canvas, $39 \times 31^1/_4''$. Collection Dr. Ferdinand Ziersch, Wuppertal-Barmen. Color plate p.111

42 *The Steamer "Odin," II.* 1927. Oil on canvas, $26^1/_2 \times 39^1/_2''$. The Museum of Modern Art, New York, acquired through the Lillie P. Bliss Bequest. Color plate p.110

GRIESHABER, H. A. P.   born 1909

43 *Elysium.* 1953. Color woodcut, $43^1/_2 \times 24^1/_4''$. The Museum of Modern Art, New York, gift of Mr. and Mrs. E. Powis Jones. Ill. p.216

GROSZ, George   born 1893

44 *Memories of New York.* 1917. Lithograph, $14^3/_4 \times 11^5/_8''$. From "Erste George Grosz-Mappe," a portfolio of 9 lithographs, published by Heinz Barger, Berlin. The Museum of Modern Art, New York, Purchase 1949. Ill. p.208

45 *Funeral of the Poet Panizza.* 1917-1918. Oil on canvas, $55^1/_8 \times 43^1/_4''$. Staatliche Kunstsammlungen, Stuttgart. Color plate p.83

46 *Café Neptun.* c.1920. Watercolor, $18^1/_2 \times 14^1/_2''$. The Art Institute of Chicago, Olivia Shaler Swan Fund. Ill. p.84

47 *Christmas Eve.* 1921. Lithograph, $18^1/_4 \times 14^1/_4''$. The Museum of Modern Art, New York, gift of Paul J. Sachs. Ill. p.215

48　*In Rue Blondel.* 1925. Watercolor, $18\,^1/_4 \times 16''$. Collection Mr. and Mrs. Erich Cohn, New York. Ill. p. 84

49　*The Poet Max Hermann-Neisse.* 1927. Oil on canvas, $23\,^3/_8 \times 29\,^1/_8''$. The Museum of Modern Art, New York, Purchase 1952. Ill. p. 85

HARTUNG, Karl　born 1908

50　*Torso.* 1950. Bronze 55'' high. Collection Andrew P. Fuller, Fort Worth, Texas. Ill. p. 181

HECKEL, Erich　born 1883

51　*Nude (Fränzi).* 1911. Color woodcut, $14\,^7/_8 \times 10\,^7/_8''$. Collection Walter Bareiss, Greenwich, Connecticut. Ill. p. 195

52　*Two Men at a Table.* 1912. Oil on canvas, $38\,^1/_4 \times 47\,^1/_4''$. Kunsthalle, Hamburg. Ill. p. 47

53　*White Horses.* 1912. Color woodcut, $12\,^1/_8 \times 12\,^3/_8''$. The Museum of Modern Art, New York, Purchase 1949. Ill. p. 191

54　*A Crystal Day.* 1913. Oil on canvas, $47\,^1/_4 \times 37\,^3/_4''$. Collection Max Kruss, Berlin. Color plate p. 48

55　*Self Portrait.* 1919. Color woodcut, $18\,^1/_4 \times 12\,^3/_4''$. The Museum of Modern Art, New York, Purchase 1950

HEILIGER, Bernhard　born 1915

56　*Head of Ernst Reuter.* 1954. Bronze, 18'' high. Collection, Kurt H. Grunebaum, Harrison, New York. Ill. p. 182

HOFER, Carl　1878–1955

57　*Three Clowns.* 1922. Oil on canvas, $51\,^1/_4 \times 41\,^3/_8''$. Wallraf-Richartz Museum, Cologne. Color plate p. 97

58　*Houses at Montagnola.* 1926. Oil on canvas, $25\,^3/_4 \times 31\,^7/_8''$. Niedersächsische Landesgalerie, Hanover. Color plate p. 98

59　*Early Hour.* 1935. Oil on canvas, $49\,^1/_4 \times 61\,^3/_8''$. Portland Art Museum, Portland, Oregon. Ill. p. 99

60　*Girl with Plant.* 1946. Lithograph, $15\,^1/_2 \times 8\,^1/_2''$. The Museum of Modern Art, New York, Purchase 1947

JAWLENSKY, Alexei von　1864-1941

61　*Still Life with Lamp.* 1906-07. Oil on cardboard, $21\,^1/_4 \times 18\,^7/_8''$. Collection Mrs. Hanna Bekker-vom Rath, Frankfurt. Color plate p. 64

62　*Egyptian Girl.* 1913. Oil on board, $21 \times 19\,^1/_2''$. Collection Mr. and Mrs. Morton D. May, St. Louis. Color plate p. 65

KANDINSKY, Wassily　1866-1944

63　*Landscape with Houses (Murnau).* 1909. Oil en board, $27\,^3/_8 \times 38''$. Kunstsammlungen der Stadt Düsseldorf. Color plate p. 67

64　*Composition.* 1913. Oil on canvas, $34\,^1/_2 \times 39\,^1/_4''$. Room of Contemporary Art, Albright Art Gallery, Buffalo, New York. Ill. p. 69

65　*Improvisation No. 30 (Warlike Theme).* 1913. Oil on canvas, $43\,^1/_4 \times 43\,^3/_4''$. The Art Institute of Chicago, Arthur Jerome Eddy Memorial Collection. Ill. p. 68

66　*Composition (3).* 1914. Oil on canvas, $64 \times 36\,^1/_4''$. The Museum of Modern Art, New York, Mrs. Simon Guggenheim Fund. Color plate p. 71

67　*Composition 8, No. 260.* 1923. Oil on canvas, $55\,^1/_2 \times 79\,^1/_8''$. The Solomon R. Guggenheim Museum, New York. Color plate p. 117

68　*Abstraction.* 1923. Color lithograph, $16 \times 15\,^1/_8''$. The Museum of Modern Art, New York, Purchase 1949. Ill. p. 211

69　*No. 678.* 1940. Oil on canvas, $39\,^1/_4 \times 25\,^1/_2''$. The Solomon R. Guggenheim Museum, New York. Ill. p. 118

KIRCHNER, Ernst Ludwig　1880–1938

70　*Dodo and Her Brother.* 1905-06. Oil on canvas, $67\,^1/_4 \times 37\,^1/_2''$. Smith College Museum of Art, Northampton, Massachusetts. Ill. p. 39

71　*Girls on the Banks of the Elbe.* c. 1910. Color lithograph, $12\,^7/_8 \times 15''$. Collection Walter Bareiss, Greenwich, Connecticut. Ill. p. 190

72　*The Street.* 1913. Oil on canvas, $47\,^1/_2 \times 35\,^7/_8''$. The Museum of Modern Art, New York, Purchase 1939. Color plate p. 40

73　*Artillerymen.* 1915. Oil on canvas, $55\,^1/_4 \times 59\,^3/_8''$. The Museum of Modern Art, New York, gift of Mr. and Mrs. Morton D. May. Ill. p. 43

74　*Market Place with Red Tower.* 1915. Oil on canvas, $47\,^1/_4 \times 35\,^5/_8''$. Folkwang Museum, Essen. Color plate p. 41

75　*Otto Mueller.* 1915. Color woodcut, $10\,^7/_8 \times 21\,^1/_2''$. Dr. Bernhard Sprengel, Hanover. Ill. p. 193

76　*Street Crossing, Leipzig.* 1915-1916. Lithograph, $23\,^1/_2 \times 20''$. Collection Walter Bareiss, Greenwich, Connecticut. Ill. p. 192

77　*Frau Dr. R. Binswanger.* 1917. Woodcut, $21\,^3/_4 \times 8\,^1/_2''$. The Museum of Modern Art, New York, Purchase 1949. Ill. p. 189

78　*Father Mueller.* 1917. Color woodcut, $21\,^7/_8 \times 13\,^3/_8''$. The Museum of Modern Art, New York, gift of Victor S. Riesenfeld

79 *Street Scene.* 1922. Color woodcut after a painting of 1914, $27^3/_4 \times 15''$. The Museum of Modern Art, New York, Purchase 1945

80 *The Painters of the Brücke.* 1925. Oil on canvas, $66^1/_8 \times 49^5/_8''$. Wallraf-Richartz Museum, Cologne. Color plate p. 44

81 *Zurich.* 1926. Oil on canvas, $53 \times 47''$. Collection Mr. and Mrs. Bruce B. Dayton, Minneapolis, Minnesota. Ill. p. 45

KLEE, Paul 1879–1940

82 *Little World.* 1914. Etching, $5^5/_8 \times 3^3/_4''$. The Museum of Modern Art, New York, Purchase 1941

83 *Destruction and Hope.* 1916. Lithograph and watercolor, $18^3/_8 \times 13''$. The Museum of Modern Art, New York, Purchase 1944. Ill. p. 210

84 *Steamer for Lugano.* 1922. Lithograph, $10^7/_8 \times 15^3/_8''$. Private collection, New York. Ill. p. 213

85 *The One in Love.* 1923. Color lithograph, $10^7/_8 \times 7^1/_2''$. From "Meistermappe des Staatlichen Bauhauses," a portfolio of 8 prints by 8 artists, published by Bauhausverlag, Munich-Weimar. The Museum of Modern Art, New York, Larry Aldrich Fund

86 *Landscape with Dam (Flussbaulandschaft).* 1924. Oil on canvas, $14^1/_8 \times 21^1/_8''$. Staatliche Kunsthalle, Karlsruhe. Color plate p. 120

87 *Fish Magic (Fischzauber).* 1925. Oil on canvas mounted on board, $30^3/_8 \times 38^1/_2''$. Philadelphia Museum of Art, Louise and Walter Arensberg Collection, Philadelphia, Pennsylvania. (Exhibited in New York only). Ill. p. 121

88 *Around the Fish (Um den Fisch).* 1926. Oil on canvas, $18^3/_8 \times 25^1/_8''$. The Museum of Modern Art, New York, Mrs. John D. Rockefeller, Jr. Fund. (Exhibited in St. Louis only). Ill. p. 122

89 *A Gay Repast (Bunte Mahlzeit).* 1928. Oil on canvas, $33^3/_8 \times 26^3/_4''$. Collection Mrs. Gabriel Hauge, Washington, D. C. Color plate p. 123

90 *Mask of Fear (Maske Furcht).* 1932. Oil on burlap, $39^1/_2 \times 22^1/_2''$. Collection Dr. and Mrs. Allan Roos, New York. Ill. p. 124

91 *Why Does He Run?* 1932. Etching, $9^3/_8 \times 11^3/_4''$. The Museum of Modern Art, New York, Purchase 1949. Ill. p. 213

92 *Revolution of the Viaduct (Revolution des Viaduktes).* 1937. Oil on canvas, $23^5/_8 \times 19^3/_4''$. Kunsthalle, Hamburg. Color plate p. 127

93 *Caprice in February (Capriccio im Februar).* 1938. Oil on canvas, $39 \times 28^1/_2''$. Collection Mr. and Mrs. Morton Neumann, Chicago. Ill. p. 126

94 *Captive (Gefangen).* 1940. Oil on burlap mounted on wood, $19^3/_4 \times 18^1/_4''$. Collection Mr. and Mrs. Frederick Zimmermann, New York. Color plate p. 128

KOKOSCHKA, Oskar   born 1886

95 *Portrait of Dr. Tietze and His Wife.* 1909. Oil on canvas, $30^1/_8 \times 53^5/_8''$. The Museum of Modern Art, New York, Mrs. John D. Rockefeller, Jr. Fund. Color plate p. 74

96 *Portrait of Herwarth Walden.* 1910. Oil on canvas, $39^1/_2 \times 27^1/_4''$. Collection Mr. and Mrs. Samuel H. Maslon, Wayzata, Minnesota (through the courtesy of the Minneapolis Institute of Arts). Color plate p. 77

97 *Dent du Midi.* 1910. Oil on canvas, $31^1/_8 \times 45^1/_4''$. Collection Mrs. W. Feilchenfeldt, Zurich, Switzerland. Ill. p. 76

98 *Man and Woman with Candle.* 1913. Lithograph, $13^1/_8 \times 10^1/_2''$. From "Der Gefesselte Columbus," a portfolio of 12 lithographs illustrating a play by the artist, published by Fritz Gurlitt, Berlin. The Museum of Modern Art, New York, given anonymously. Ill. p. 202

99 *Man and Woman Standing in Room.* 1913. Lithograph, $14^1/_2 \times 10^1/_2''$. From "Der Gefesselte Columbus," a portfolio of 12 lithographs illustrating a play by the artist, published by Fritz Gurlitt, Berlin. The Museum of Modern Art, New York, Purchase 1951

100 *Wanderer.* 1914. Lithograph, $16^3/_8 \times 12^3/_8''$. From "Bachkantate: O Ewigkeit, Du Donnerwort," a portfolio of 11 lithographs, published by Fritz Gurlitt, Berlin. The Museum of Modern Art, New York, Purchase 1947. Ill. p. 202

101 *The Power of Music (Die Macht der Musik).* 1919. Oil on canvas, $40^1/_8 \times 59''$. Stedelijk van Abbe-museum, Eindhoven, Holland. Ill. p. 79

102 *Self Portrait.* 1923. Color lithograph, $24^1/_2 \times 18^3/_8''$. The Museum of Modern Art, New York, Purchase 1952. Ill. p. 203

103 *London Bridge: View of the Thames.* 1925-26. Oil on canvas, $35^5/_8 \times 51^1/_4''$. Room of Contemporary Art, Albright Art Gallery, Buffalo, New York. Color plate p. 81

KOLBE, Georg 1877-1947

104 *Assunta.* 1921. Bronze, 6' 3" high. The Detroit Institute of Arts, Detroit, Michigan. Ill. p. 163

KOLLWITZ, Käthe 1867-1945

105 *Plowmen.* 1905. Etching with pencil corrections, $17^{1}/_{2} \times$ 23″. Unique proof of 3rd state. Collection Walter Bareiss, Greenwich, Connecticut. Ill. p. 187

106 *Death Reaching into a Group of Children.* 1934. Lithograph, $19^{1}/_{2} \times 16^{1}/_{2}$″. From "Tod", a series of 8 lithographs. The Museum of Modern Art, New York, Purchase 1940

LEHMBRUCK, Wilhelm 1881-1919

107 *Standing Woman.* 1910. Bronze (cast 1916-17). 6′ 4″ high. City Art Museum of St. Louis, Missouri. (Exhibited in St. Louis only). Ill. p. 157

108 *Kneeling Woman.* 1911. Cast stone, $69^{1}/_{2}$″ high. The Museum of Modern Art, New York, Mrs. John D. Rockefeller, Jr. Fund. (Exhibited in New York only). Ill. p. 159

109 *Standing Youth.* 1913. Cast stone, 7′ 8″ high. The Museum of Modern Art, New York, gift of Mrs. John D. Rockefeller, Jr. (Exhibited in New York only). Ill. p. 161

110 *Bowing Female Torso.* 1913. Terra cotta, $35^{1}/_{2}$″ high. Collection Mr. and Mrs. Morton D. May, St. Louis, Missouri. (Exhibited in St. Louis only). Ill. p. 158

111 *Macbeth.* 1918. Etching and drypoint, $15^{1}/_{2} \times 11^{3}/_{4}$″. The Museum of Modern Art, New York, Mrs. John D. Rockefeller, Jr. Fund. Ill. p. 207

MACKE, August 1887—1914

112 *The Dress Shop.* 1913. Oil on canvas, $19^{7}/_{8} \times 23^{5}/_{8}$″. Collection Mrs. Gisela Macke, Bonn. Color plate p. 62

113 *Girls under Trees.* 1914. Oil on canvas, $47^{1}/_{4} \times 63$″. Kunsthaus, Zurich, Switzerland, on loan from private collection. Color plate p. 63

MARC, Franz 1880—1916

114 *Fighting Cows.* 1911. Oil on canvas, $32^{3}/_{4} \times 54$″. Private collection, New York. (Exhibited in New York only). Ill. p. 55

115 *Blue Horses.* 1911. Oil on canvas, $41^{3}/_{8} \times 71^{3}/_{8}$″. Walker Art Center, Minneapolis, Minnesota. Color plate p. 56

116 *Tigers.* 1912. Woodcut, $7^{7}/_{8} \times 9^{1}/_{2}$″. From "Buch der Toten," a special issue of the periodical "Die Dichtung," published by Roland-Verlag, Munich. The Museum of Modern Art, New York, Purchase 1951. Ill. p. 200

117 *Deer in a Flower Garden.* 1913. Oil on canvas, $21^{5}/_{8} \times 29^{7}/_{8}$″. Kunsthalle, Bremen. Color plate p. 59

118 *Tyrol.* 1913-1914. Oil on canvas, $53^{3}/_{8} \times 57$″. Bayerische Staatsgemäldesammlungen, Munich. Ill. p. 60

MARCKS, Gerhard born 1889

119 *Two Cats.* 1921. Woodcut, $9^{3}/_{8} \times 15^{1}/_{4}$″. From "Erste Mappe: Meister des Staatlichen Bauhauses in Weimar," a portfolio of 14 prints by 7 artists, published by the Bauhaus, Weimar. The Museum of Modern Art, New York, gift of Mrs. Donald B. Straus

120a *Maja.* 1942. Bronze, 89″ high. Collection Nelson A. Rockefeller, New York. (Exhibited in New York only). Ill. p. 168

   b *Maja.* 1942. Bronze, 89″ high. City Art Museum of St. Louis, Missouri. (Exhibited in St. Louis only)

121 *Bat.* 1948. Woodcut, $8^{5}/_{8} \times 9$″. The Museum of Modern Art, New York, gift of Mrs. Donald B. Straus. Ill. p. 201

122 *Melusine III.* 1949. Bronze, $43^{1}/_{2}$″ high. Walker Art Center, Minneapolis, Minnesota. Ill. p. 168

MATARÉ, Ewald born 1887

123 *Young Bull.* 1923. Mahogany, $18^{1}/_{2} \times 24^{3}/_{4}$″. Saarland Museum, Saarbrücken. Ill. p. 172

124 *Nocturnal Pasture.* 1925. Color woodcut, $7^{5}/_{8} \times 17^{5}/_{8}$″. The Museum of Modern Art, New York, gift of Edgar Kaufmann, Jr.

125 *Standing Figure* 1926—1927. Walnut, $21^{5}/_{8}$″ high. Collection Dr. Hugo Häring, Biberach an der Riss. Ill. p. 173

MODERSOHN-BECKER, Paula 1876—1907

126 *Blind Woman in the Forest.* 1900. Etching, $6^{1}/_{4} \times 5^{1}/_{2}$″. The Museum of Modern Art, New York, Larry Aldrich Fund

127 *Head of a Peasant Girl.* 1900. Etching, $4 \times 5^{1}/_{2}$″. The Museum of Modern Art, New York, Larry Aldrich Fund

128 *Old Peasant Woman.* 1906-1907. Oil on canvas, $30^{1}/_{4} \times 22^{1}/_{2}$″. Private collection, U.S.A. Ill. p. 29

129 *Self Portrait (with Camellia).* 1907. Oil on board, $23^{5}/_{8} \times 11$″. Folkwang Museum, Essen. Color plate p. 28

MUELLER, Otto 1874—1930

130 *Woods.* c. 1915. Color lithograph, $9^{7}/_{8} \times 6^{3}/_{4}$″. Collection Walter Bareiss, Greenwich, Connecticut

131 *Two Bathers.* c. 1919? Color lithograph, $10 \times 6^{1}/_{2}$″. The Museum of Modern Art, New York, given anonymously

132 *Three Girls in the Woods.* c. 1920. Oil on burlap, 48×53″. Collection Mr. and Mrs. Morton D. May, St. Louis, Missouri. Color plate p. 52

selected bibliography

The following 230 references offer a representative cross-section of the relevant literature, emphasizing, within the available space, items most directly related to the exhibition. Many of these titles contain additional bibliographical citations. For convenience the material has been grouped as follows: *General* (1-34), *Movements and Groups* (35-79), *Painting* (80-92), *Sculpture* (93-103), *Graphics* (104-117), *Individual Artists* (118-222).

Nancy Riegen, Reference Librarian

GENERAL
Books

1   BARR, Alfred H., Jr. Cubism and Abstract Art. 249p. ill. New York, Museum of Modern Art, 1936. *"Abstract Expressionism in Germany"*, p. 64-72.

2   BURGER, Fritz. Einführung in die moderne Kunst. 136p. ill. Berlin, Athenaion, 1917.

3   EINSTEIN, Carl. Die Kunst des 20. Jahrhunderts. 3d. ed. 655p. ill. Berlin, Propyläen Verlag, 1931. *1st ed. 1926; 2d ed. 1931.*

4   GROTE, Ludwig. Deutsche Kunst im zwanzigsten Jahrhundert. 2d. rev. ed. 151p. ill. Munich, Prestel, 1954. *1st ed. 1953, based on the 1953 Lucerne exhibition of German art. See bibl. 20.*

5   HILDEBRANDT, Hans. Die Kunst des 19. und 20. Jahrhunderts. 458p. ill. Wildpark-Potsdam, Athenaion, 1924.

6   HUYGHE, René, ed. L'Allemagne et l'Europe centrale. *In* Huyghe, René, ed. Histoire de l'Art contemporain. Paris, Alcan, 1935. ch. 16 p. 417-446 ill. *Bibliographies. Partial contents: "L'Impressionisme et l'Expressionisme en Allemagne" par Paul Westheim. — "L' Art non-figuratif en Allemagne" par Will Grohmann. — "La Peinture de l'Allemagne inquiète" par Fritz Schiff.*

7   RAYNAL, Maurice, ed. The History of Modern Painting. 3 v. ill. Geneva, Skira, 1949-50. *Vol. 2. "Matisse, Munch, Rouault: Fauvism, Expressionism" contains sections on Die Brücke and Expressionism with chapters on Modersohn-Becker, Kirchner, Schmidt-Rottluff, Kandinsky, Jawlensky, Nolde and Kokoschka; vol. 3. "From Picasso to Surrealiam" contains chapters on the Blaue Reiter, Kandinsky, Marc, Klee and the Bauhaus. Bibliographies by Hans Bolliger; special expressionist bibliography in German edition of vol. 2.*

8   READ, Herbert. Art Now: an introduction to the theory of modern painting and sculpture, rev. and enl. ed. 144p. ill. London, Faber and Faber, 1948.

9   SAUERLANDT, Max. Die Kunst der letzten 30 Jahre. 208p. ill. Berlin, Rembrandt, 1935. *2d ed. Hamburg, Laatzen, 1948.*

10   SCHMIDT, Paul Ferdinand. Jüngste Entwicklung. *In his* Kunst der Gegenwart. p. 84-127 ill. Wildpark-Potsdam, Athenaion, 1923.

11   THIELE, Ernst. Die Situation der Bildenden Kunst in Deutschland. 143p. Stuttgart, Cologne, Kohlhammer, 1954. *Partial contents: Die Situation der Bildenden Kunst in Deutschland von Eduard Trier. — Sammlungen und Ausstellungen zeitgenössischer Kunst von Kurt Martin. — Deutsches Schrifttum zur zeitgenössischen Kunst im Spiegel der Presse.*

12   THIEME, Ulrich *and* BECKER, Felix. Allgemeines Lexikon der Bildenden Künstler. 37 v. Leipzig, Seemann, 1907-1950. *Supplemented by VOLLMER, Hans. Allgemeines Lexikon der Bildenden Künstler des XX. Jahrhunderts. In progress. 3 v. pubd. Leipzig, Seemann, 1953-current.*

13   THOENE, Peter, pseud. Modern German Art. 108p. ill. Harmondsworth, Middlesex, England, Penguin Books, 1938.

14   SCHEFFLER, Karl. Geschichte der europäischen Malerei vom Impressionismus bis zur Gegenwart. Geschichte der europäischen Plastik im neunzehnten und zwanzigsten Jahrhundert. 348p. ill. Berlin, Cassirer, 1927.

15   WESTHEIM, Paul. Für und Wider: kritische Anmerkungen zur Kunst der Gegenwart. 192p. ill. *A collection of essays on art and artists including Hofer, Barlach, Beckmann, Schmidt-Rottluff, Mueller, Rohlfs, Grosz and Belling.*

16 WESTHEIM, Paul. Helden und Abenteuer: Welt und Leben der Künstler. 238p. ill. Berlin, Reckendorf, 1931. *A collection of essays on various artists including Marc, Nolde, Kirchner, Klee and Dix.*

Catalogues

17 BUCHHOLZ GALLERY, NEW YORK. Catalogues, 12v. ill. New York, Curt Valentin, 1938-1955. *A partial record, bound by exhibition seasons, of the catalogues of this gallery which included joint and individual shows of German artists, notably Klee, Feininger and Beckmann. (Set in Museum of Modern Art Library).*

18 JUSTI, Ludwig. Von Corinth bis Klee. 206p. ill. Berlin, Bard, 1931. *Deutsche Malkunst im 19. und 20. Jahrhundert: ein Gang durch die Nationalgalerie.*

19 KESTNER GESELLSCHAFT, HANNOVER. [Exhibition catalogues] ill. Hanover, 1916-current. *Numerous collective and individual shows of German artists, e.g. no.37, Lehmbruck (1920), no.138, Paula Modersohn-Becker (1934), Deutsche Bildhauer der Gegenwart (1951).*

20 LUCERNE. KUNSTMUSEUM. Deutsche Kunst: Meisterwerke des 20. Jahrhunderts. 64p. ill. Munich, Prestel, 1953. *Edited by Ludwig Grote in collaboration with Leonie von Wilckens.*

21 NEW HAVEN. YALE UNIVERSITY. ART GALLERY. Collection of the Société Anonyme: Museum of Modern Art 1920. 223p. ill. New Haven, 1950. *Collection presented by Katharine S. Dreier and Marcel Duchamp. Catalogue edited by G. H. Hamilton. Numerous biographical notes on German artists.*

22 NEW YORK. MUSEUM OF MODERN ART. German Painting and Sculpture. 43p. ill. New York, 1931. *Introduction by A.H. Barr, Jr.*

23 NEW YORK. MUSEUM OF MODERN ART. The New Decade: 22 European Painters and Sculptors. 111p. ill. New York, 1955. *Text by A.C. Ritchie. Includes Uhlmann, Werner, Winter. Bibliography.*

24 TURIN. MUSEO CIVICO. Expressionismo e Arte tedesca del 20. Secolo. Dipinti, sculture, disegni del Museo Wallraf-Richartz... Colonia. 76p. ill. Turin, 1954. *Preface by Leopold Reidemeister.*

Series

25 JUNGE KUNST. [Reihe.] Leipzig, Klinkhardt & Biermann, 1921-30. *Partial contents: Pechstein.- Paula Modersohn-Becker.- Klee.- Schmidt Rottluff.- Grosz.- Macke.- Rohlfs.- Dix.- Kandinsky.- Feininger.- Hofer.- Kokoschka.- Nolde.- Beckmann.- Sintenis. Most of these originally pubd. in Jahrbuch der jungen Kunst (Leipzig) and Cicerone (Leipzig).*

26 PIPER - BUCHEREI. Munich, Piper, 1943-current. *Partial contents: no.74. Max Beckmann der Zeichner; no.75. Franz Marc: Botschaften an den Prinzen Jussuff; no.80. Christian Rohlfs: Blätter aus Ascona; no.84. Wilhelm Lehmbruck: Zeichnungen und Radierungen; no.89. Oskar Kokoschka: Lithographien; no.90. Ernst Wilhelm Nay: Aquarelle. Picture books with brief introductory text.*

27 KUNSTWERK-SCHRIFTEN. Baden-Baden, Klein, 1950-current. *Partial contents: Bd.13. Deutsche Graphik der Gegenwart; Bd.19/20. Abstrakte Kunst: Theorien und Tendenzen; Bd.22. Deutsche Bildhauer der Gegenwart; Bd.23. Futuristen – Expressionisten; Bd.26. Deutsche Zeichner der Gegenwart; Bd.42. Deutsche Malerei der Gegenwart; Bd.43/44. Abstrakte Kunst. Separate issues of Das Kunstwerk on special subjects.*

Special Numbers of Periodicals

28 ART D'AUJOURD'HUI, Aug. 1953
Ser.4, no 6:1-27, titled "L'art abstrait en Allemagne d'aujourd' hui." Contains articles on the Blaue Reiter and the Bauhaus by Ludwig Grote and notes on 18 contemporary German abstract artists, including Baumeister, Nay, Uhlmann, Winter and Werner.

29 THE ATLANTIC, no.3, 1957
Special number on Germany. Contains article by A. S. Vellinghausen titled "Art as evidence of freedom: contemporary painting, sculpture and architecture." p.127-145, ill.

30 DOCUMENTS, 1951/1952
German contemporary art: a special issue published by the Gesellschaft für übernationale Zusammenarbeit. 106p. ill. Offenburg in Baden, Dokumente-Verlag, 1952. *Published successively in French, German, and English. Contains chapters on Expressionism, the Blaue Reiter, the Bauhaus, Beckmann, Kokoschka and Macke; twelve contributors.*

Selected Articles

31 LINDAU, ROM. Modern movements in German art. *The Arts* (New York) 14, no.1:24-30, ill. July 1928.

32 ROH, Franz. L'art contemporain en Allemagne. *Prisme des Arts* 8:19-26 ill. Jan. 1957.

33 WEIDLER, Charlotte. Art in Western Germany today. *Magazine of Art* 44, no.4:132-137 ill. Apr. 1951.

34 ZAHN, Leopold. Deutsche Kunst der Gegenwart. *Das Kunstwerk* 2, no.1/2:55-65 ill. 1948.

MOVEMENTS AND GROUPS

Expressionism

35 FECHTER, Paul. Der Expressionismus. 56p. ill. Munich, Piper, 1914.

36 GASCH, Sebastian. El Expresionismo. 47p. ill. Barcelona, Omega, 1955. *Largely pictorial.*

37 GROHMANN, Will. Évolution et rayonnement de l'expressionisme. *XXe Siècle* new ser. 4:18-24 ill. Jan. 1954.

38 GROHMANN, Will. Expressionisten. 77p. ill. Munich etc. Desch, 1956. *A picture book.*

39 HAUSENSTEIN, Wilhelm. Über Expressionismus in der Malerei. 2d ed. 76p. Berlin, Reiss, 1919.

40 HESS, Hans. German expressionism. *Art* (London) 1 no. 8:5. Mar. 3, 1956.

41 HILDEBRANDT, Hans. Der Expressionismus in der Malerei. 27p. Stuttgart and Berlin, Deutsche Verlags-Anstalt, 1919.

42 HODIN, Joseph Paul. The Dilemma of Being Modern: essays on art and literature. 271p. ill. London, Routledge & Kegan Paul, 1956. *Part two: The Expressionists.*

43 KESSLER, Charles S. Sun worship and anxiety: nature nakedness and nihilism in German Expressionist painting. *Magazine of Art* 45:304-12 ill. Nov. 1952.

44 LANDSBERGER, Franz. Impressionismus und Expressionismus. 47p. ill. Leipzig, Klinkhardt & Biermann, 1921.

45 LORCK, Carl von. Expressionismus: Einführung in die europäische Kunst des 20. Jahrhunderts. 63p. ill. Lübeck, Wildner, 1947.

46 MINNESOTA. UNIVERSITY. UNIVERSITY GALLERY. German Expressionism in Art: painting, sculpture, prints, 1905-1935. 34p. Minneapolis, 1950. *Foreword by R. L. (i.e. Ruth E. Lawrence). Bibliography.*

47 MYERS, Bernard. Expressionism in German Painting: a generation in revolt. ill. New York, Praeger, 1957. *Also foreign editions. Extensive bibliography and documentation.*

48 NEUMAYER, Heinrich. Expressionismus. 15p. ill. Vienna, Rosenbaum, 1956. *A picture book.*

49 SAMUEL, Richard. Expressionism in German Life, Literature and the Theatre (1910-1924). Studies by Richard Samuel and R. Hinton Thomas. 203p. ill. Cambridge, Eng., Heffer, 1939. *Bibliography.*

50 SCHMALENBACH, Fritz. Grundlinien des Frühexpressionismus. *In his* Kunsthistorische Studien. p.49-99. Basel, 1941.

51 SELZ, Peter. German Expressionist Painting. 647 leaves ill. 1954. *Unpublished thesis. Bibliography Rev. ed. in preparation to be pubd. by the University of California Press (1958?).*

52 SYDOW, Eckart von. Die deutsche expressionistische Kultur und Malerei. 151p. ill. Berlin, Furche, 1920. *Bibliography.*

53 VALENTINER, W.R. Expressionism and abstract painting *The Art Quarterly* 4, no. 3:210-239 ill. Summer 1941.

54 WALDEN, Herwarth, *ed.* Expressionismus: die Kunstwende. 142p. ill. Berlin, Der Sturm, 1918.

Die Brücke

55 APOLLONIO, Umbro. "Die Brücke" e la Cultura dell'Espressionismo. 102p. ill. Venice, Alfieri, 1952. *Bibliography.*

56 BERNE. KUNSTHALLE. Die Brücke. 32p. ill. Berne, Kunsthalle, 1948. *Contains material on Paula Modersohn-Becker as well as on the Brücke artists Heckel, Kirchner, Mueller, Nolde, Pechstein and Schmidt-Rottluff. Bibliography.*

57 BUCHHEIM, Lothar-Günther. Die Künstlergemeinschaft Brücke: Gemälde, Zeichnungen, Graphik, Plastik, Dokumente. 408p. ill. Feldafing, Buchheim-Verlag, 1956. *Separate chapters on the members of the Brücke: Heckel, Kirchner, Schmidt-Rottluff, Mueller, Pechstein and Nolde. Bibliography.*

58 HAENDLER, Gerhard. "Die Bruecke." *Arts Plastiques* 5, no.6:419-426 ill. June/July 1952. *Text in French.*

59 SCHMIDT, Paul Ferdinand. Blütezeit der Dresdener Brücke: Erinnerungen. *Aussaat* 2, no.1-2:49-55, ill. 1947.

Der Blaue Reiter

60 GROHMANN, Will. The Blue Rider. *In* Bernier, Georges and Rosamond, *eds.* The Selective Eye. p.26-35 ill. New York, Reynal, 1956. *Translation of article originally pubd. in French in the magazine "L'Oeil," no.9:4-13 Sept. 1955.*

61 KANDINSKY, Wassily & MARC, Franz, *eds.* Der Blaue Reiter. 131p. ill. Munich, Piper, 1912. *2d ed., 1914, with revised text.*

62 MUNICH. HAUS DER KUNST. Der Blaue Reiter: München und die Kunst des 20. Jahrhunderts, 1908-1914. 45p. ill. Munich-Pasing, Filser, 1949. *Exhibition catalogue. Introduction by Ludwig Grote. Contains extracts from the writings of Klee, Kandinsky and Marc. Supplemented by* BASEL KUNSTHALLE. *Der Blaue Reiter, 1908-14: Wegbereiter und Zeitgenossen. Basel, 1950.*

63 THWAITES, John Anthony. The Blaue Reiter, a milestone in Europe. *The Art Quarterly* 13, no. 1:2-21 ill. Winter 1956.

Der Sturm

64 HOFFMANN, Edith. "Der Sturm", a document of expressionism. *Signature new ser., no. 18: 44-55 ill. 1954.*

65 SCHREYER, Lothar. Erinnerungen an Sturm und Bauhaus. 295p. ill. Munich, Langen, Müller, 1956. *Contains chapters on Kokoschka, Schwitters, Feininger, Klee, Schlemmer and Kandinsky.*

66 DER STURM. Wochenschrift für Kultur und Künste. Berlin 1910-1932. *Edited by Herwarth Walden.*

67 STUTTGARTER KUNSTKABINETT, STUTTGART. (Catalogue of 20th Auction). 165p. ill. Stuttgart, 1954. *Partial contents: Sammlung Nell Walden ("Der Sturm").*

68 WALDEN, Nell and SCHREYER, Lothar, eds. Der Sturm: ein Erinnerungsbuch an Herwarth Walden und die Künstler aus dem Sturmkreis. 275p. ill. Baden-Baden, Klein, 1954.

Neue Sachlichkeit

69 READ, Herbert. "Die neue Sachlichkeit." *In his* Art now. rev. & enl. ed. p. 84-87. London, Faber & Faber, 1948.

70 ROH, Franz. Nach-Expressionismus: magischer Realismus. 134p. ill. Leipzig, Klinkhardt & Biermann, 1925.

71 SCHMALENBACH, Fritz. Der Name "neue Sachlichkeit." *In his* Kunsthistorische Studien. p. 22-32. Basel, 1941. *Supplemented by "Jugendstil und neue Sachlichkeit," p. 9-21.*

72 SCHMALENBACH, Fritz. The term "neue Sachlichkeit." *Art Bulletin*, 22 no. 3: 161-5, Sept. 1940.

Bauhaus

73 BAUHAUS: Zeitschrift für Gestaltung, Dessau, 1926-1929, 1931. *Editors: Gropius and Moholy-Nagy, 1926-1928; Meyer and Kállai, 1929; Hilbersheimer, Albers, Kandinsky, 1931.*

74 BAUHAUS, WEIMAR. Staatliches Bauhaus, Weimar, 1919-1923. 225p. ill. Weimar, Munich, 1923.

75 BAYER, Herbert *and others.* Bauhaus, 1919-1928, ed. by Herbert Bayer, Walter Gropius, Ilse Gropius. 224p. ill. New York, Museum of Modern Art, 1938. *Reprint: Boston, Branford, 1952. Originally published on occasion of the Bauhaus exhibition at the Museum of Modern Art, New York, Dec. 1938-Jan. 1939. Bibliography includes a list of Bauhaus publications.*

76 BILL, Max. The Bauhaus idea: from Weimar to Ulm. *In* Architects' Year Book, no. 5. p. 29-32 ill. London, Elek. 1953.

77 EMGE, C. A. Die Idee des Bauhauses: Kunst und Wirklichkeit. 35p. Berlin, Pan, Heise, 1924.

78 GIEDION, Sigfried. Walter Gropius and the Bauhaus. *In his* Walter Gropius: Work and Teamwork. p. 27-44 ill. New York, Reinhold, 1954.

79 MUNICH. HAUS DER KUNST. Die Maler am Bauhaus. 56p. ill. Munich, Prestel, 1950. *Exhibition catalogue. Contains material on Kandinsky, Klee, Schlemmer, Feininger and Marcks. Introduction by Ludwig Grote.*

PAINTING

80 DERI, Max. Die Malerei im XIX. Jahrhundert. 2v. ill. Berlin, Cassirer, 1923. *Supplemented by his Die neue Malerei. 151p. ill. Leipzig, Seemann, 1921.*

81 DOMINICK, Ottomar. Die schöpferischen Kräfte in der abstrakten Malerei. 134p. ill. Bergen, Müller & Kiepenheuer, 1947. *Ein Zyklus mit F. Winter, O. Ritschl, W. Baumeister, M. Ackermann, G. Meistermann.*

82 GEROLD, Karl Gustav. Deutsche Malerei unserer Zeit. 229p. ill. Vienna etc., Desch, 1956.

83 HAFTMANN, Werner. German abstract painters. *College Art Journal*, 14, no. 4: 332-339 ill. Summer 1955.

84 HAFTMANN, Werner. Malerei im 20. Jahrhundert. 2v. ill. Munich, Prestel, 1954. *Contains chapters on the various movements in German art, on Paula Modersohn-Becker, Nolde, Rohlfs, Marc, Macke, Klee, Jawlensky, Kokoschka, Kandinsky, Beckmann, Hofer, Schlemmer, Feininger, Baumeister and Ernst. Vol. 1, Text. – 2, Pictorial supplement.*

85 HANDLER, Gerhard. German painting in our time. 201p. ill. Berlin, Rembrandt, 1956. *Also German edition.*

86 HULFTEGGER, Adeline. Evolution de la Peinture en Allemagne et en Europe centrale des Origines à nos Jours. 350p. ill. Paris, Horizons de France, 1949. *Bibliography.*

87 LONDON. TATE GALLERY. A hundred years of German painting. 30p. ill. London, 1956. *Exhibition catalogue. Introduction by Alfred Hentzen.*

88 NEMITZ, Fritz. Deutsche Malerei der Gegenwart. 129p. ill. Munich, Piper, 1948. *Contains chapters on Marc, Kandinsky, Klee, Beckmann, Hofer, Kokoschka, Die Brücke, Kirchner, Schmidt-Rottluff, Heckel, Mueller, Pechstein and Nolde.*

89 RÖTHEL, Hans Konrad. Moderne deutsche Malerei. 101p. ill. Wiesbaden, Vollmer, 1957, *Bibliographies.*

90 SCHMIDT, Paul Ferdinand. Geschichte der modernen Malerei. 275p. ill. Zurich, Fretz & Wasmuth, 1952. *"Deutsche Malerei" p. 156-238. Fourth ed. issued by Kohlhammer, Stuttgart 1954 (279p.). Includes bibliography.*

91 WALDMANN, Emile. La Peinture allemande contemporaine. 73p. ill. Paris, Crès, 1930.

92 WILD, Doris. Moderne Malerei: ihre Entwicklung seit dem Impressionismus 1880-1953. 261p. ill. Constance, Europa, 1950.

SCULPTURE

93 GIEDION-WELCKER, Carola. Contemporary Sculpture: an evolution in volume and space. 327p. ill. New York, Wittenborn, 1955. *Also German edition. Revised and enlarged edition of "Moderne Plastik": Elemente der Wirklichkeit, Masse und Auflockerung, Zurich, 1937. Bibliographies.*

94 GERTZ, Ulrich. Plastik der Gegenwart. 224p. ill. Berlin, Rembrandt, 1953. *Plate section – "Plastik in Deutschland:" p.41-158.*

95 HAMBURG. ALSTERPARK. Plastik im Freien, hrsg. von Carl Georg Heise. 64p. ill. Munich, Prestel, 1953. *Catalogue and biographical notes, p.11-16. Also supplementary exhibition catalogue, 30p., with preface by W. Haftmann.*

96 HENTZEN, Alfred. Deutsche Bildhauer der Gegenwart. 118p. ill. Berlin, Rembrandt, 1934. *Contains material on Barlach, Belling, Kolbe, Lehmbruck, Marcks, Mataré, Sintenis, Stadler and others. Supplemented by Kestner-Gesellschaft. Deutsche Bildhauer der Gegenwart, Hanover 1951. Exhibition catalogue. Preface by Hentzen.*

97 HILDEBRANDT, Hans. Deutsche Plastik der Gegenwart. Werk 39:265-72 Aug. 1952.

98 KUHN, Alfred. Die neuere Plastik von Achtzehnhundert bis zur Gegenwart. 134p. ill. Munich, Delphin, 1922. *Material on Lehmbruck, Barlach and Belling.*

99 NEMITZ, Fritz. Junge Bildhauer. 79p. ill. Berlin, Rembrandt, 1939. *Mainly pictorial.*

100 RAVE, Paul Ortwin. Deutsche Bildnerkunst von Schadow bis zur Gegenwart. 230p. ill. Berlin, Bard, 1929. *Ein Führer zu den Bildwerken der National-Galerie. Includes chapters on Kolbe, Lehmbruck, Barlach and Belling.*

101 RITCHIE, Andrew Carnduff. Sculpture of the Twentieth Century. 238p. ill. New York, Museum of Modern Art, 1952. *Bibliography.*

101a SCHAEFER-SIMMERN, Henry. Sculpture in Europe Today. 33p. ill. Berkeley and Los Angeles, University of California Press, 1955. *Brief text; pictorial supplement.*

102 TRIER, Eduard. Moderne Plastik von Auguste Rodin bis Marino Marini. 102p. ill. Frankfurt am Main, Büchergilde Gutenberg, 1955. *Bibliography.*

103 WERNER, Bruno E. Die Deutsche Plastik der Gegenwart. 214p. ill. Berlin, Rembrandt, 1940.

GRAPHICS

104 BUCHHEIM BUCHER, Feldafing, Buchheim, 1945-current. *Picture books on Kokoschka, Beckmann, Kirchner, Der Blaue Reiter, graphics, etc.*

105 CELLE. SCHLOSS. Von Klinger bis Beckmann: deutsche Graphik von 1880 bis 1930. 56p. ill. Celle, 1952. *Exhibition catalogue. Introduction by Lothar Pretzell.*

106 DUSSELDORF. STÄDT. KUNSTSAMMLUNGEN. Expressionistische und nachexpressionistische Druckgraphik. 56p. ill. Dusseldorf, 1953. *Text by Werner Doede. A picture book.*

107 GLASER, Curt. Graphik der Neuzeit. 584p. ill. Berlin, Cassirer, 1923.

108 GÖPEL, Erhard. Deutsche Holzschnitte des XX.Jahrhunderts. 55p. ill. Wiesbaden, Insel-Verlag, 1955. *A picture book.*

109 HARTLAUB, G. F. Die Graphik des Expressionismus in Deutschland. 69p. ill. Stuttgart und Calw, Hatje, 1947.

110 KUNSTWERK, vol. 4, no. 2 1950. 64p. ill. *Special issue titled "Moderne deutsche Graphik." Partial contents: Moderne deutsche Graphik – ein Überblick von Leopold Zahn. – Der moderne Holzschnitt von Rudolf Schröder. – Geschnittene Poesie-Holzschnitte von E. Mataré, von A. Schulze-Vellinghausen. – Omnia vana [Kokoschka] von H. M. Wingler.*

111 PFISTER, Kurt. Deutsche Graphiker der Gegenwart. 41p. ill. Leipzig, Klinkhardt & Biermann, 1920.

112 POMMERANZ-LIEDTKE, Gerhard. Der graphische Zyklus von Max Klinger bis zur Gegenwart. 226p. ill. Berlin, Deutsche Akademie der Künste, 1956.

113 ROSENBERG, Jakob. German expressionist printmakers. *Magazine of Art 38, no. 8:300-305 ill. Dec. 1945.*

114 SCHIEFLER, Gustav. Meine Graphik-Sammlung. 66p. ill. Hamburg, Gesellschaft der Bücherfreunde, 1927. *Contains sections on Nolde and the other artists of the Brücke group.*

115 SCHRÖDER, Rudolf. Deutsche Holzschneider. 132p. ill. Duisburg, Drei Eulen Verlag, 1948. *Mainly pictorial.*

116 WEDDERKOP, H. von. Deutsche Graphik des Westens. 200p. ill. Weimar, Feuerverlag, 1922. *Includes chapters on Rohlfs, Lehmbruck, Macke and Beckmann.*

117 ZIGROSSER, Carl. The Expressionists: a survey of their graphic art. 37p. ill. New York, Braziller, 1957. *Text with pictorial supplement.*

INDIVIDUAL ARTISTS

Barlach

118 BERLIN, DEUTSCHE AKADEMIE DER KÜNSTE. Ernst Barlach. Ausstellung, Dez. 1951-Feb. 1952. 187p. ill. Berlin 1951. *Bibliography. Supplemented by GIELOW, Wolfgang. Ernst Barlach: Literaturverzeichnis. 27p. Munich, Gielow, 1954.*

119 CARLS, Carl Dietrich. Ernst Barlach: das plastische, graphische und dichterische Werk. 6. Aufl. 142p. ill. Berlin, Rembrandt, 1954, *1st ed. 1931.*

120 DROSS, Friedrich, *ed.* Ernst Barlach: Leben und Werk in seinen Briefen, 268p. ill. Munich, Piper, 1952

Baum

121 LEONHARD, Kurt. Der Bildhauer Otto Baum. *Kunstwerk* 2 no. 10:36-38 ill. 1948.

122 ROH, Franz. Otto Baum. 34p. ill. Tübingen, Reichl, 1950. *Text in German, English and French.*

Baumeister

123 GROHMANN, Will. Willi Baumeister. 60p. ill. Stuttgart, Kohlhammer, 1952. *Text in German, French and English. Bibliography.*

124 SÉLECTION. Chronique de la vie artistique XI: Willi Baumeister. 60p. ill. Antwerp, Editions Sélection, 1931. *Text by W. Grohmann, Flouquet, G. Waldemar and others.*

Beckmann

125 BECKMANN, Max. Tagebücher 1940-50. 429p. ill. Munich, Langen, 1955. *Arranged by Mathilde Q. Beckmann. Edited by Erhard Göpel.*

126 GLASER, Curt *and others.* Max Beckmann. 87p. ill. Munich, Piper, 1924.

127 REIFENBERG, Benno and HAUSENSTEIN, Wilhelm. Max Beckmann. 82p. ill. Munich, Piper, 1949.

128 ST. LOUIS. CITY ART MUSEUM. Max Beckmann, 1948. 114p. ill. St. Louis, 1948. *Exhibition catalogue. Introduction by Perry T. Rathbone. Extensive bibliography.*

129 SOBY, James Thrall. Max Beckmann. *In his* Contemporary Painters. p. 85-91, ill. New York, Museum of Modern Art, 1948.

Belling

130 KUHN, Alfred. Rudolf Belling. *In his* Neuere Plastik von Achtzehnhundert bis zur Gegenwart. p. 121-123, ill. Munich, Delphin, 1922.

131 WESTHEIM, Paul. Rudolf Belling. *In his* Für und Wider. p. 187-195, ill. Potsdam, Kiepenheuer, 1923.

Blumenthal

132 HEISE, C. G. Empfindung und Gestaltung: zu neueren Arbeiten des Bildhauers Hermann Blumenthal. *Die Kunst* (Munich) 79:340-4 ill. Aug. 1939.

133 ISERMEYER, Christian-Adolf. Der Bildhauer Hermann Blumenthal. 14p. ill. Berlin, Mann, 1947.

Corinth

134 KUHN, Alfred. Lovis Corinth. 215p. ill. Berlin, Propyläen-Verlag, 1925.

135 OSTEN, Gert von der. Lovis Corinth. 124p. ill. Hanover, Kunstverein; Munich, Bruckmann, 1955. *Bibliography.*

Dix

136 BARR, Alfred Hamilton, Jr. Otto Dix. *Arts* (New York) 17:234-51 ill. Jan. 1931.

137 WESTHEIM, Paul. Dix: Steckbrief als Malmethode. *In his* Helden und Abenteuer: Welt und Leben der Künstler. p. 228-232 ill. Berlin, Reckendorf, 1931.

Ernst

138 ERNST, Max. Beyond Painting and Other Writings by the Artist and his Friends. 204p. ill. New York, Wittenborn, Schultz, 1948. *Bibliography.*

139 BRUHL. SCHLOSS AUGUSTBURG. Max Ernst: Gemälde und Graphik, 1920-1950. 97p. ill. Brühl, 1951. *Catalogue published on the occasion of an exhibition to celebrate Ernst's 60th birthday. Bibliography.*

140 WALDBERG, Patrick. Le rire de Max Ernst. *XXe Siècle* new ser. no. 8:17-20 ill. Jan. 1957.

Feininger

141 BOSTON. INSTITUTE OF CONTEMPORARY ART. Jaques Villon. Lyonel Feininger. 46p. ill. New York, Chanticleer Press, 1950. *Lyonel Feininger by Frederick S. Wight, p. 28-43. Bibliography.*

142 NEW YORK. MUSEUM OF MODERN ART. Lyonel Feininger, with essays by Alois J. Schardt and Alfred H. Barr, Jr., and excerpts from the artist's letters. Edited by Dorothy C. Miller... 96p. ill. New York, 1944. *Catalogue of joint Feininger-Hartley exhibition. Feininger, p. 6-52. Bibliography.*

Grieshaber

143 KESTNER GESELLSCHAFT, HANNOVER. H. A. P. Grieshaber. 13p. ill. Hanover, 1954. *Exhibition catalogue. Introduction by Herbert Herrmann.*

144 STUTTGART. WÜRTTEMBERGISCHER KUNSTVEREIN. H A. P. Grieshaber. Otto Baum. 22p. ill. Stuttgart, 1954. *Catalogue of joint exhibition in the Kunstgebäude, Stuttgart. Text by Egon Vietta and Franz Roh.*

Grosz

145 BALLO, Ferdinand. Grosz. 79p. ill. Milan, Rosa e Ballo, 1946.

146 GROSZ, George. A little Yes and a big No: the Autobiography of George Grosz. 272p. ill. New York, Dial Press, 1946.

147 NEW YORK. WHITNEY MUSEUM OF AMERICAN ART. George Grosz. 67p. ill. New York, 1954. *Exhibition catalogue. Text by John I. H. Baur. Bibliography.*

Hartung

148 BERLIN. HAUS AM WALDSEE. Karl Hartung. Ausstellung. 22p. ill. Berlin, 1952. *Preface by K. L. Skutsch.*

149 KESTNER GESELLSCHAFT, HANNOVER. Karl Hartung. 14p. ill. Hanover, 1953. *Exhibition catalogue. Text by A. Hentzen.*

Heckel

150 RAVE, Paul Ortwin. Erich Heckel. 6p. ill. Leipzig, Volk und Buch Verlag, 1948.

151 THORMAEHLEN, Ludwig. Erich Heckel. 19p. ill. Karlsruhe, Akademie der Bildenden Künste und die Staatliche Kunsthalle, 1953. *Speech by Thormaehlen at the opening of the Erich Heckel exhibition in Karlsruhe on 23. Sept. 1950.*

Heiliger

152 FLEMMING, Hanns Theodor. Der Bildhauer Bernhard Heiliger. *Die Kunst und das schöne Heim* 55, no. 2: 52-55 ill. Nov. 1955.

153 SKUTSCH, Karl Ludwig. Bernhard Heiliger. *Zeitschrift für Kunst,* 14 no. 2: 149-151, 153-160 ill. 1950.

Hofer

154 HOFER, Karl. Erinnerungen eines Malers. 230p. Berlin-Grunewald, Herbig, 1953.

a HOFER, Karl. Über das Gesetzliche in der Bildenden Kunst. 180p. ill. Berlin, Akademie der Künste, 1956.

155 JANNASCH, Adolf. Carl Hofer. 15p. ill. Potsdam, Stichnote, 1948.

a RUMPEL, H. Karl Hofer. *Werk* 35 no. 11: 353-60 ill. Nov. 1946.

Jawlensky

156 GROHMANN, Will. L'évolution de la figure chez Jawlensky. *Cahiers d'art* no. 5: no. 5-8; 193-196 ill. 1934.

157 WEILER, Clemens. Alexej von Jawlensky, der Maler und Mensch. 47p. ill. Wiesbaden, Limes, 1955. *Short bibliography.*

Kandinsky

158 BILL, Max, ed. Wassily Kandinsky. 178p. ill. Boston, Institute of Contemporary Art. 1951. *A collection of essays by various contributors. Contains English, German and Spanish translations of text. Also pubd. without translations by Maeght, Paris, 1951. Bibliography.*

a EICHNER, Johannes. Kandinsky und Gabriele Münter: von Ursprüngen moderner Kunst. 221p. ill. Munich, Bruckmann, 1957.

159 GROHMANN, Will. Kandinsky. ill. Cologne, DuMont Schauberg, New York, Abrams. [1958]. *German and English editions in progress; extensive bibliographies.*

160 KANDINSKY, Wassily. Concerning the Spiritual in Art. 95p. ill. Wittenborn, Schultz, 1947. *Other editions: Munich, Piper, 1912; London, Constable, 1914; New York, Guggenheim Foundation, 1946.*

161 KANDINSKY, Wassily. Kandinsky: Essays über Kunst und Künstler, hrsg. und kommentiert von Max Bill. 247p. ill. Stuttgart, Hatje, 1955.

Kirchner

162 GROHMANN, Will. Das Werk Ernst Ludwig Kirchners. 55p. ill. Munich, Wolff, 1926.

163 [KIRCHNER, Ernst Ludwig]. Zeichnungen von E. L. Kirchner. *Genius* (Munich) 2: 216-234 ill. 1920. *Supplemented by "Über Kirchners Graphik." Genius 3: 251-263 ill. 1921. Both articles signed L. de Marsalle (pseud. of E. L. Kirchner).*

164 MYERS, Bernhard. Ernst Ludwig Kirchner and "Die Brücke." *Magazine of Art* 45: 20-26 ill. Jan. 1952.

165 SCHIEFLER, Gustav. Die Graphik Ernst Ludwig Kirchners. 2v. ill. Berlin, Euphorion, 1924-31.

166 STUTTGART. WÜRTTEMBERGISCHER KUNSTVEREIN. Ausstellung E. L. Kirchner 1880-1938: Gemälde, Aquarelle, Zeichnungen, Graphik. 24p. ill. Stuttgart, 1956. *Exhibition catalogue. Foreword by E. Rathke. Bibliography.*

Klee

167 GROHMANN, Will. Paul Klee. 447p. ill. New York, Abrams, 1954. *Bibliography. Also German edition.*

168 HAFTMANN, Werner. The Mind and Work of Paul Klee. 68p. ill. New York, Praeger, 1954. *Bibliography. Also German edition.*

169 HULTON, Nika. An Approach to Paul Klee. 68p. ill. New York, Pitman, 1956.

170 KLEE, Paul. Das bildnerische Denken. Hrsg. und bearbeitet von Jürg Spiller. 541p. ill. Basel, Stuttgart, Schwabe, 1956.

171 KLEE, Paul. Tagebücher von Paul Klee 1898-1918. 423p. ill. Cologne, DuMont Schauberg, 1957. *Edited by Felix Klee.*

Kokoschka

172 BOSTON. INSTITUTE OF CONTEMPORARY ART. Oskar Kokoschka: a retrospective exhibition. 87p. ill. New York, Chanticleer Press, 1948. *Introduction by James S. Plaut. Selected bibliography.*

173 HOFFMANN, Edith. Kokoschka, Life and Work, 367p. ill. Boston, Boston Book & Art Shop, 1947. *Contains two essays by Kokoschka and a foreword by Herbert Read.*

a KOKOSCHKA, Oskar. Schriften, 1907-1955. 484p. ill. Munich, Langen, Müller, 1956. *Arranged and edited with explanatory and bibliographic text by Hans Maria Wingler.*

174 WINGLER, J. Hans Maria. Oskar Kokoschka: das Werk des Malers. 401p. ill. Salzburg, Galerie Welz, 1956. *Bibliography.*

Kolbe

175 GRAFLY, Dorothy. Lederer and Kolbe. *Magazine of Art* 26:115-126 ill. Mar. 1933.

176 PINDER, Wilhelm. Georg Kolbe: Werke der letzten Jahre. 84p. ill. Berlin, Rembrandt, 1937.

Kollwitz

177 KLIPSTEIN, August. The Graphic Work of Käthe Kollwitz. 359p. ill. New York, Galerie St. Etienne, 1955.

178 KOLLWITZ, Hans, ed. The Diary and Letters of Käthe Kollwitz. 200p. ill. Chicago, Regnery, 1955. *Translated by Richard and Clara Winston.*

179 ZIGROSSER, Carl. Käthe Kollwitz. 26p. ill. New York, Bittner, 1946.

Lehmbruck

180 BERNE, KUNSTHALLE. Lehmbruck, Macke, Marc. 21p. ill. Berne, 1949. *Bibliographies.*

181 HOFF, August. Wilhelm Lehmbruck: seine Sendung und sein Werk. 117p. ill. Berlin, Rembrandt, 1936.

182 DUSSELDORF. KUNSTSAMMLUNGEN DER STADT DUSSELDORF. Wilhelm Lehmbruck. 49p. ill. Düsseldorf, 149. *Exhibition catalogue. Bibliography.*

183 TRIER, Eduard. Wilhelm Lehmbruck: Paris 1910-1914. In Jahresring 55/56. p. 144-153, ill. Stuttgart, Deutsche Verlags-Anstalt, 1955.

Macke

184 HOLZHAUSEN, Walter. August Macke. 29p. ill. Munich, Bruckmann, 1956. *Short bibliography.*

185 MUNSTER. LANDESMUSEUM FÜR KUNST UND KULTURGESCHICHTE. August Macke: Gedenkausstellung zum 70. Geburtstag. 98p. ill. Münster, 1957. *Text by Hans Eichler, Herbert Schade, Max Imdahl, Walter Holzhausen, Carl Bänfer.*

186 VRIESEN, Gustav. August Macke. 306p. ill. Stuttgart, Kohlhammer, 1953. *Bibliography.*

Marc

187 LANKHEIT, Klaus. Franz Marc. Hrsg. von Maria Marc. 78p. ill. Berlin, Lemmer, 1950.

188 SCHARDT, Alois J. Franz Marc. 176p. ill. Berlin, Rembrandt, 1936. *Bibliography.*

Marcks

189 MINNEAPOLIS. WALKER ART CENTER. Gerhard Marcks. 23p. ill. Minneapolis, 1953. *Exhibition catalog. Bibliography.*

190 THIESS, Frank. Gerhard Marcks — ein Bildhauer von europäischer Größe. *Thema* (Munich) 3:29-36 ill. 1949. *The entire issue is illustrated by the works of Marcks.*

Mataré

191 FLEMMING, Hanns Theodor. Ewald Mataré. 79p. ill. Munich, Prestel, 1955. *Bibliography.*

192 TRIER, Eduard. Ewald Mataré. 23p. ill. Cologne, Seemann, 1956.

Modersohn-Becker

193 MARTEN, Lu. Paula Modersohn-Becker. *Bildende Kunst,* 1, no. 2:11-14 ill. 1947.

194 PAULI, Gustav. Paula Modersohn-Becker. 87p. ill. Berlin, Wolff, 1919.

Mueller

195 TROEGER, Eberhard. Otto Mueller. 30p. ill. Freiburg/Br., Crone, 1949.

196 WESTHEIM, Paul. Otto Mueller. *In his* Für und Wider. Potsdam. Kiepenheuer, 1923. p.120-127 ill.

Nay

197 GROHMANN, Will. E.W.Nay. *Cahiers d'art*, 27 no.2:219-225 ill. Dec. 1952.

198 HESS, Walter. Ernst Wilhelm Nay. *Die Kunst und das schöne Heim*, 54 no.7:248-251, ill. Apr. 1956.

Nolde

199 GOSEBRUCH, Martin. Nolde: Aquarelle und Zeichnungen. 74p. ill. Munich, Bruckmann, 1957.

200 HAFTMANN, Werner. Radierungen von Emil Nolde, hrsg. von Rudolf Hoffmann, mit Einleitung von Werner Haftmann. 85p. ill. Bremen, Hertz, 1948. *Supplemented by HAFTMANN. Holzschnitte von Emil Nolde, 1947 and by HAFTMANN. Die Lithographien Emil Noldes. In Jahresring 55/56. p.154-170 ill. Stuttgart, Deutsche Verlags-Anstalt, 1955.*

201 HAMBURG, KUNSTVEREIN. Gedächtnisausstellung Emil Nolde. Hamburg, 1957. *Catalogue of exhibition April-June 1957. Introduction by Alfred Hentzen.*

202 NOLDE, Emil. Jahre der Kämpfe. 242p. ill. Berlin, Rembrandt, 1934. *Supplemented by NOLDE. Das eigene Leben. Berlin 1931.*

203 SAUERLANDT, Max. Emil Nolde. 85p. ill. Munich, Wolff, 1921. *Supplemented by bibl. 9, p.72-135.*

204 SCHIEFLER, Gustav. Das graphische Werk Emil Noldes bis 1910. 139p. ill. Berlin, Bard, 1911. *Supplemented by his Das graphische Werk . . . 1910-1925. 172p. ill. Berlin, Euphorion, 1927.*

Rohlfs

205 VOGT, Paul. Christian Rohlfs. 23p. ill. Cologne, Seemann, 1956.

206 WESTHEIM, Paul. Christian Rohlfs. *In his* Für und Wider. p.128-136 ill. Potsdam, Kiepenheuer, 1923.

Schlemmer

207 HILDEBRANDT, Hans. Oskar Schlemmer. 152p. ill. Munich, Prestel, 1952. *Bibliography.*

208 HILDEBRANDT, Hans. Oskar Schlemmer. *Magazine of Art* 43:23-28 ill. Jan. 1950.

Schmidt-Rottluff

209 GROHMANN, Will. Karl Schmidt-Rottluff. 324p. ill. Stuttgart, Kohlhammer, 1956. *Bibliography.*

210 WESTHEIM, Paul. Schmidt-Rottluff. *In his* Für und Wider. p.111-119 ill. Potsdam, Kiepenheuer, 1923.

Schwitters

211 KESTNER GESELLSCHAFT, HANNOVER. Kurt Schwitters. 51p. ill. Hanover, 1954. *Exhibition catalogue. Preface by Werner Schmalenbach. Chronology by Hans Bolliger.*

212 MOTHERWELL, Robert, The Dada Painters and Poets. p. xxi-xxiv, 162-164, 275-276, 368-372, ill. New York, Wittenborn, Schultz, 1951. *Bibliography. Includes translation of "Merz" from "Der Ararat" 2:3-10, 1921.*

213 SCHWITTERS, Kurt. Merz. Hanover, 1923-1932. *Periodical edited by the artist, with numerous illustrations and contributions.*

Sintenis

214 JANNASCH, Adolf. Renée Sintenis. 64p. ill. Potsdam, Stichnote, 1949. *Mainly pictorial.*

215 KIEL, Hanna. Renée Sintenis. 112p. ill. Berlin, Rembrandt, 1956.

Stadler

216 SCHMIDT, Paul Ferdinand. Toni Stadler. *Das Kunstwerk* 5 no.2:22-25 ill. 1951.
See also bibl. 96.

Uhlmann

217 SCHIFF, Gert. Hans Uhlmann. *Art d'Aujourd'hui* ser. 4, no.6:16 ill. Aug, 1953.

218 SEEL, Eberhard. Hans Uhlmann. *Das Kunstwerk* 4 no.8/9: 81-82 ill. 1950.

Werner

219 GROHMANN, Will. Theodor Werner. *Cahiers d'Art* 24:149-158 ill. 1949.

220 SCHIFF, Gert. Theodor Werner. *Art d'Aujourd'hui* ser. 4 no.6:19 ill. Aug. 1953.

Winter

221 GROHMANN, Will. Fritz Winter. *Cahiers d'Art* 28 no.1:141-3 ill. 1953.

222 HAFTMANN, Werner. Fritz Winter: 12 Farbtafeln. 17p. ill. Berne, Marbach, 1951.

photograph credits

index

Artists whose works are illustrated in the text appear in small capitals. Illustrations are italicized under the names of artists, with the disignation (col) to indicate color illustrations.

Dorothy Simmons